AEI's BUDGET AND
RESOURCE ALLOCATION
PROJECTION MODEL

AEI's BUDGET AND RESOURCE ALLOCATION PROJECTION MODEL

Paul N. Courant • William H. Branson
Attiat F. Ott • Roy A. Wyscarver

American Enterprise Institute for Public Policy Research
Washington, D.C.

The coauthors of this volume are PAUL N. COURANT, assistant professor of economics, University of Michigan, WILLIAM H. BRANSON, professor of economics and international affairs, Woodrow Wilson School of Public and International Affairs, Princeton University, ATTIAT F. OTT, professor of economics, Clark University, and ROY A. WYSCARVER, economist, Office of Tax Analysis, U.S. Treasury, formerly of Clark University.

September 1973

ISBN 08447-3110-2

Library of Congress Catalog Card No. L.C. 73-86356

FOREWORD

AEI's Long Range Budget Projection Project was initiated in the spring of 1972 to undertake a major study of the long-run outlook for the federal budget. This study places particular emphasis on the impact of existing budget commitments on this outlook, and on possible budget savings to be realized from re-examining the rationale and efficiency of major existing and proposed programs. This monograph is the third publication to result from the study. The first was *Nixon, McGovern, and the Federal Budget,* by David J. Ott, Lawrence J. Korb, Thomas Gale Moore, Attiat F. Ott, Rudolph G. Penner and Thomas Vasquez, and the second was *Public Claims on U.S. Output: Federal Budget Options in the Last Half of the Seventies,* by the same authors. The LRBP project is directed by David J. Ott.

CONTENTS

INTRODUCTION

The AEI long-run budget projection model was developed for the purpose of examining the effects of different federal government budget policies on the allocation of resources in the U.S. economy. While the model was prepared as part of the AEI Long Range Budget Projection Project (LRBP),* it was also designed to have a wider application. The model which is described in the following pages can be used to study the allocative effects of any budget policy that the user wants to study. Indeed, perhaps the most novel feature of this report is that it includes the computer program in which the model is embodied.

The purpose of this volume is twofold. First, it presents a detailed report on the techniques and assumptions underlying the analysis in the AEI studies cited below. Second, it is intended as a guide to students of public policy who may wish to conduct budget policy studies of similar scope, but with different assumptions. As programmed, the model is a flexible tool for analyzing the long-run impacts of budget policy. It is presented here in the hope that others will use it for that purpose.

The AEI budget model is not designed to be a forecasting model. Its purpose is to investigate the course of broad economic aggregates that would be consistent with given budgetary policies of the federal government. The data generated by the model thus does not represent a *prediction* about what will occur. Rather, it is meant to indicate what would happen, under specified federal budget policies, if other sectors of the U.S. economy behaved much as they have done in the past. One of the major uses of the model, then, is to find out what allocations of private sector GNP will be consistent with different government policies.

Chapter 1 of this study presents the general method which was used in building the model. Considerable space is devoted to discussion of the national income and product accounts (NIA) structure, since the NIA provides the basic framework of the model. In addition, Chapter 1 explains in detail the purposes of the model and describes in more general terms the methods that were used to achieve those purposes.

Chapter 2 presents a detailed description of the model—the individual equations, their construction, and their purposes. Chapter 3 provides a detailed description of how to use the computer program in which the model is embodied. (The program itself is presented in an appendix.) In addition, Chapter 3 presents the results of the Nixon administration budget "run" of the model and explains how the output is interpreted.

---

*See David J. Ott, Lawrence J. Korb, Thomas Gale Moore, Attiat F. Ott, Rudolph G. Penner, and Thomas Vasquez, *Nixon, McGovern, and the Federal Budget* (Washington, D.C.: American Enterprise Institute for Public Policy Research, 1972), and *Public Claims on U.S. Output: Federal Budget Options in the Last Half of the Seventies* (Washington, D.C.: American Enterprise Institute, 1973). The latter is referred to hereafter as the "Options Volume."

Chapter 1
AN OVERVIEW OF THE AEI MODEL

Any long-term budget projection model has to be an integral part of a larger model projecting gross national product (GNP) and its major categories, in terms of both output and income. The revenue side of the budget, as well as some expenditures like unemployment compensation, will depend on the state of the economy during the projection period. Also, if the assumption is made that the economy will follow some particular GNP path—perhaps full-employment GNP—then the budget projections must be consistent with that path so that total projected demand adds up to projected GNP. The AEI model is an attempt to provide a consistent set of estimates of the major categories of GNP that add up to full-employment GNP. This provides a framework for analysis of long-run budget problems.

This chapter is devoted to a general description of the AEI model. First is a brief discussion of the basic accounting framework of the model—the NIA. The next section is a description of the procedures for projecting the demand components of GNP, assuming GNP is at its full-employment level. The following section discusses budget policy required to insure that total demand adds up to full-employment GNP. Finally, the role of monetary policy in a full-employment budget projection model is analyzed.

The Framework for the AEI Budget Model

The NIA provide a natural framework and structure for a model of long-term resource allocation, the basic purpose of the AEI budget model. The accounts measure GNP in terms of output or product of the economy, and in terms of the income generated by that production. These two measures—which must add up to the same total, GNP in current dollars—are referred to below as the "product side" measure and the "income side" measure. One useful way to view a long-term model of the economy is as a projected set of accounts which is internally consistent and adds up to full-employment GNP on both product and income sides. The government expenditures and revenues that are part of such a set of projected accounts are then consistent with full employment, and substantial deviations from these levels of expenditures, if not offset by changes in tax revenues, would be expected to result in either inflation or unemployment. Thus the budget model will bring out the fact that in its budget decisions the federal government is not simply budgeting its own resources; it is budgeting GNP.

Since changes in the budget projections affect the composition of GNP by affecting, directly or indirectly, the components of GNP on the product or income side, a brief discussion of the major components and their orders of magnitude might be useful as an introduction to the AEI budget model.[1]

Table 1 shows the breakdown by major categories of GNP on the product side. This breakdown can be expressed as part of the GNP identity that is familiar from the beginning economics course:

$$GNP = C + I + G + (X - M),$$

where C is personal consumption expenditures, I is gross private domestic investment, G is total government purchases of goods and services, and $(X - M)$ is net exports. In the budget projections discussed later, it will be seen that two major product-side components that are directly affected by the budget are personal consumption expenditures and federal government purchases of goods and services. If, with a given projection of all other product-side demand categories, projected total product-side demand adds up to more than projected full-employment GNP, the budget can be used to reduce demand either by reducing government purchases or by increasing personal taxes and/or reducing transfer payments, thus reducing consumption spending.

Table 1
GROSS NATIONAL PRODUCT AND ITS MAJOR COMPONENTS, 1971
($ in billions)

Gross national product	$1,050
Personal consumption expenditures	665
Gross private domestic investment	152
Business fixed investment	106
Residential structures	43
Change in business inventories	4
Net exports of goods and services	1
Government purchases of goods and services	233
Federal	98
State and local	135

Source: *Survey of Current Business,* July 1972.

Part of the flow of payments for GNP—the purchases of the product-side categories—does not show up as income to producers. The main deductions are capital consumption allowances—depreciation of the nation's capital stock—and indirect business taxes, sales or excise taxes that reduce the payment received by the seller below that paid by the buyer. The translation of GNP into national income (NI) is shown in Table 2, along with the distribution of national income by type of income.

Table 2

GROSS NATIONAL PRODUCT BY TYPE OF INCOME, 1971

($ in billions)

Gross national product	$1,050[a]
Less: Capital consumption allowances	94
Net national product	957
Less: Indirect business taxes	102
Business transfer payments	5
Statistical discrepancy	-5
Plus: Net subsidies to government enterprises	1
National income	856
Compensation of employees	644
Proprietors' income	70
Rental income of persons	25
Corporate profits	79
Net interest	39

[a]Figures do not add due to rounding.
Source: *Survey of Current Business,* July 1972.

The other, more interesting way to look at the income side of the accounts is to study the allocation of income among tax payments (T), savings (S), private transfers payments abroad (R), and personal consumption expenditures (C). This distribution of income is shown in Table 3, which can be expressed as the other familiar identity from the accounts,

$$GNP = C + S + T + R.$$

Here an important link between the income and product sides is clear. Personal consumption expenditures appear as the main use of income on the income side and the main component of output on the product side. In terms of the previous example, if total product-side demand is projected to exceed full-employment GNP, then personal tax payments can be raised, reducing consumption expenditures on both income and product sides.

Total GNP and its product-side components are calculated in both current and constant (1958) dollar values. Thus, for GNP and the major demand categories, an *implicit* deflator—a GNP price index—can be calculated by dividing the current dollar value by the constant dollar value. In the budget projections, both constant and current dollar product-side data are calculated.

The constant dollar estimates on the product side are compiled by deflating current dollar data at subcategory levels by various price indexes for commodities. Such indexes are not calculated for income-side categories. Indeed, such an index is quite fuzzy conceptually; presumably the proper deflator for dividends, for example, depends on what they are spent on, and this leads back to product-side categories.

Table 3

ALLOCATION OF GROSS NATIONAL PRODUCT ON THE INCOME SIDE, 1971

($ in billions)

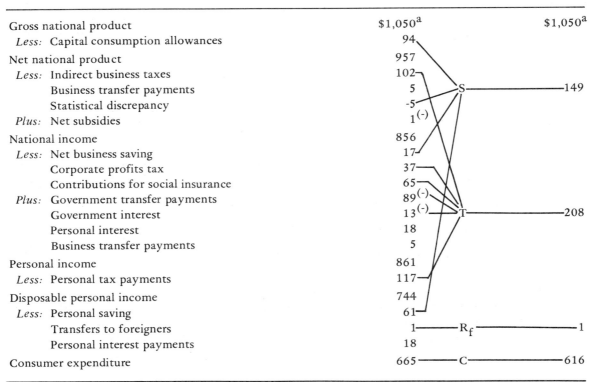

Gross national product	$1,050[a]	$1,050[a]
Less: Capital consumption allowances	94	
Net national product	957	
Less: Indirect business taxes	102	
Business transfer payments	5	S — 149
Statistical discrepancy	-5	
Plus: Net subsidies	1 (-)	
National income	856	
Less: Net business saving	17	
Corporate profits tax	37	
Contributions for social insurance	65	
Plus: Government transfer payments	89 (-)	
Government interest	13 (-)	T — 208
Personal interest	18	
Business transfer payments	5	
Personal income	861	
Less: Personal tax payments	117	
Disposable personal income	744	
Less: Personal saving	61	
Transfers to foreigners	1 — R_f — 1	
Personal interest payments	18	
Consumer expenditure	665 — C — 616	

[a] Figures do not add due to rounding.

Source: *Survey of Current Business,* July 1972.

However, since personal consumption appears on both the income and product sides, it is frequently deflated by the consumer price index (CPI) or the personal consumption expenditures implicit delfator (PCED). In the projections below, an estimate of real (constant dollar) consumption expenditures is, in fact, obtained by deflating personal consumption expenditures (PCE) by PCED.

The total government sector—federal, state, and local—in the accounts is shown in Table 4. These entries must be consistent with the product and income side as shown in Tables 1 and 3. It is important to notice that the item for government purchase of goods and services, $233 billion, is about two-thirds of total expenditures by governments. Government purchases of currently produced goods and services are the only expenditure item appearing on the product side of the accounts. These purchases represent the government's "draft" on the economy's real output.

Table 4

GOVERNMENT SECTOR IN THE NATIONAL INCOME AND PRODUCT ACCOUNTS, 1971

($ in billions)

Expenditures		Receipts	
Purchases of goods and services	$233	Personal tax	$117
Transfer payments	92	Corporate profits tax	37
To persons	89	Indirect business tax	102
To foreigners	3	Contributions for social insurance	65
Net interest	13		
Net subsidies	1		
Total expenditures	339	Total receipts	321

Source: *Survey of Current Business,* July 1972.

The rest of expenditures must be netted against total receipts to obtain net tax revenue (T) on the income side of the accounts. Transfers "to persons," interest, and subsidy payments are negative tax payments from the national income accountant's point of view. These payments put tax receipts back into the income stream, redistributing after-tax income from persons paying taxes (positive) to those receiving transfer, interest, or subsidy payments.[2]

The federal government part of the government sector in the accounts is shown in Table 5. Except for the grants-in-aid entry in Table 5, the items in that table can be subtracted from those in Table 4 to obtain the state and local government share of the government sector. Grants-in-aid are federal government grants to state and local governments, which are expenditures in the federal budget and receipts in the state and local budgets. These cancel out when the two are aggregated into the total government sector.

Table 5

FEDERAL GOVERNMENT SECTOR IN THE NATIONAL INCOME AND PRODUCT ACCOUNTS, 1971

($ in billions)

Expenditures		Receipts	
Purchases of goods and services	$ 98	Personal tax	$ 90
Transfer payments	75	Corporate profits tax	33
To persons	72	Indirect business tax	20
To foreigners	3	Contributions for social insurance	56
Grants-in-aid	29		
Net interest	14		
Net subsidies	5		
Total expenditures	221	Total receipts	199

Source: *Survey of Current Business,* July 1972.

The federal sector in the NIA is what is referred to as "the budget" in the analysis and projections that follow. It is the items in this budget, mainly government purchases and personal income tax receipts, that are the instruments that the government can use to maintain total demand on the product side of the accounts roughly equal to full-employment GNP. And it is the surplus or deficit in NIA terms that is meant when we refer to the projected budget surplus. This surplus will be calculated as a result of the GNP-budgeting procedure, rather than being a target in itself. Again, the exercise in long-term budget allocation models is budgeting full-employment GNP, not budgeting an expenditure total that must equal tax revenues.

Projecting Full-Employment Demand in the AEI Budget Model

The basic idea behind the model is quite simple.[3] To a first approximation, supply or potential output (GNP) in a year 197X will be determined by labor force and productivity growth. Total demand in the economy, by private consumers and businesses, state and local governments, and the federal government is then calculated and must roughly equal potential GNP (supply). If it exceeds supply, inflation results; if it falls short, unemployment is produced.

Given an initial level of demand which produces full employment without inflation, if one element of spending—say federal purchases—rises, another element—say consumer spending—must be reduced. This can be achieved by raising tax rates. Thus the "trade-off" can be expressed in terms of one kind of spending versus another, or in terms of the tax changes needed to achieve the required private spending level.

The model's calculations can be viewed in three steps. First, potential GNP is calculated. Total demand is then computed, with no tax changes and an assumed level of government spending. Then the excess (or deficit) of total demand over potential supply is calculated. This can then be converted into the expenditure cut (or increase) or tax increase (or reduction) needed to bring demand into line with supply. This tax or spending change, added to normal tax revenue growth and the previously assumed government spending level, yields the budget surplus (or deficit) needed to maintain full employment without inflation.

Full-Employment Output. Full-employment is defined in the AEI model in terms of the unemployment rate. The projections in the "Options Volume" are discussed under alternative assumptions about what constitutes full employment, namely, unemployment rates of 4 percent, of 4½ percent and 5 percent. That is, the model allows the user to pick his own definition of full employment. At the same time, the model incorporates a variant of "Okun's Law,"[4] in that for every percentage point the unemployment rate exceeds 4 percent, real GNP is reduced by about 3 percent. This reflects the notion that as unemployment rises above 4 percent, some workers drop out of the labor force, causing a sharper drop in the GNP than would otherwise occur.

Given the chosen unemployment rate, output will increase due to increases in the size of the labor force and in the average productivity of the labor force. Projections of labor force growth are available from a number of sources, both public and private. At full employment, productivity is assumed to increase at a rate of 3 percent per year in the private sector, and to remain constant in the public sector.[5] This is a noncontroversial assumption, and underlies a number of past studies involving projection of the growth of GNP.[6] The projection of labor force growth through 1980 is also quite straightforward, as it is essentially independent of assumptions about the birth rate, all members of the projected labor force already having been born.

Once projections of private sector productivity and total employment have been made, all that is necessary to project potential GNP is to allocate total employment between the private and public sectors. In the context of the AEI model, this is done in the process of projecting the federal, state and local budgets, as discussed in Chapter 2.

Projecting the rate of inflation that is consistent with the unemployment rate used to define full employment is more difficult. Recent econometric studies suggest that an inflation rate of about 4 percent per year (measured in terms of the increase in the GNP implicit deflator [GNPD]) would accompany 4 percent unemployment in the absence of price controls.[7] Given this evidence, and the objective of the Nixon administration to hold the inflation rate down to around 2.5 percent, the "Options Volume" presents projections with a 2.5 percent inflation rate assumption but with "alternative" full-employment definitions of 4 to 5 percent unemployment.

In any case, this problem does not create great difficulties for long-term budget projections. Whatever the unemployment rate used to define full employment, a higher rate of inflation than assumed increases both estimated potential GNP in current dollars and projected demand in current dollars by approximately the same amount, leaving the balance unchanged. The projections are made in "real" terms—in 1971 dollars—and an inflation assumption is then used to convert the results into estimated current dollars.

The growth in potential output computed by the method discussed above provides a supply of output, potential real GNP. The long-run budget problem is then to hold total demand roughly equal to potential output.

Business Investment Demand. In the long-term budget model the path of investment must be consistent with the assumed growth of GNP. The basic assumption made is that investment will expand enough to hold the aggregate ratio of capital stock to private output constant. This means that, at full employment, business fixed investment, in real terms, will absorb about 11-12 percent of real private GNP each year. This fraction is very close to that obtained by the Office of Business Economics in the Department of Commerce from simulated runs of their medium-term econometric model.[8]

In addition, to keep inventory stocks growing in line with final sales, inventory investment is assumed to absorb another 1 percent of real private-sector output, so that total business investment is projected to absorb about 12 percent of real private GNP.

These projections implicitly assume a monetary policy that adjusts to obtain these investment ratios—an "accommodating" monetary policy consistent with the implied investment path (including residential construction, discussed below). The fiscal, or budget, policy problem is for the federal government to set the combined levels of its own purchases and of consumer spending (through tax policy) so that they add up to the total output remaining after investment and state and local government purchases are deducted from GNP.[9]

Residential Construction. The basic assumption behind any projection of residential construction investment is the projected path of annual housing starts. The ratio of expenditures in residential construction in 1958 dollars to annual starts—roughly the average real cost per unit—has remained very steady at about $15,500 since the late 1950s. With no particular reason to expect this to change during the 1970s, the projected number of starts is simply multiplied by $15,500 to obtain projections of expenditures for residential construction in 1958 dollars.

Housing starts are a strongly cyclical variable, with large increases in recessions when credit becomes easy and large drops when credit tightens in cyclical upswings. Total starts for the year 1972 were around 2.2 million. As the recovery continues in 1973 and the economy moves back toward full employment, starts can be expected to drop to perhaps 2.0 million. In the projection period 1975-80, with steady growth in GNP assumed, housing starts could be expected to grow gradually in the absence of unusual monetary policy activity or stimulus from the federal government. The residential construction projections here thus assume steady growth in housing starts from 2.3 million in 1975 to 2.5 million in 1980.

State and Local Government Purchases. State and local government purchases, in constant dollars, are divided into purchases for elementary and secondary education, purchases for higher education, and other purchases. In 1972, the first category accounted for $42.6 billion, or 32 percent of total purchases, and the second category accounted for $12.0 billion, or 8.9 percent of total purchases.[10] Spending in each of the three categories is assumed to change over time as the populations they serve change and as changes occur in the real per-capita level of services. Population changes are assumed to be those reported in Census Series E-1 for the educational categories, and Census Series E for the overall population.[11] Real per-capita levels of services are assumed to increase at the same average rate as they did in the years 1954-71.

Thus, for each of the three categories, 1971 dollar expenditure in year X is equal to 1971 expenditure, times an index of population change, times an index of the projected change in the per-capita level of services. Conversion of the projections into current dollars is discussed in Chapter 2.

Net Exports. By 1972 the traditional net export surplus of the United States had disappeared, to be replaced by a deficit of about $5 billion for the year 1972. The new economic policy announced by the President in August 1971 aimed at eliminating that deficit. The exchange rate realignments agreed upon in December 1971 and early 1973 should have this desired effect by the beginning of our projection period. One recent estimate of the effects of the 1971 realignment, which effectively devalued the dollar by some 6 percent, was an $8 billion swing in the U.S. trade surplus.[12] This estimate may have been too optimistic, but the more recent devaluation should help to take up any slack. Overall, given that it is U.S. policy to avoid deficits in the balance of trade, and also that the causes of the recent deficit are not likely to disappear soon, it seemed reasonable to assume that exports will approximately equal imports during the projection period.

Personal Consumption Expenditures. Table 3 shows that PCE is basically derived from the income side of the NIA. GNP is assumed to follow the projected full-employment path. Since the income-side data are in current dollars only, real potential GNP must be multiplied by an assumed value of the GNP deflator to obtain current dollar full-employment GNP.[13] The reason for inflating the GNP estimate to nominal terms is that all of the items on the income side "between" GNP and disposable personal income (DPY) are estimated in nominal terms, there being no "real" income-side data.

Once we have nominally projected full-employment GNP, we can make the additions and deductions shown in Table 3 to get to DPY. These are estimated by a series of fairly simple econometric equations and a set of more sophisticated tax equations discussed in Chapter 2 and Appendix A below. Notice that two major tax deductions are made in going from GNP to DPY: indirect business taxes and personal income taxes.

Next, the estimate of nominal DPY can be multiplied by the projected fraction of income that goes to consumer spending to obtain the projected path of PCE. (This is then deflated by the implicit PCE deflator to get real PCE.) A very important question is: What fraction of DPY will go to PCE?

The sum of personal interest plus private transfers to foreigners has been a very steady 2.5 percent of DPY since 1965. Thus the question is how to allocate the remaining 97.5 percent of DPY between personal saving and personal consumption expenditure. In Chapter 2 below, the argument is made that a best guess for the saving ratio in the projection period is about 7.0 percent. This leaves 90.5 percent of DPY going to PCE.

The crucial nature of this assumption, and the importance of continuing research in saving behavior, is evident from the following consideration. If, for example, the projected saving ratio is increased by one point to 8.0 percent (the consumption ratio is lowered to 89.5 percent), some $10 billion is subtracted from projected demand in 1975 (1 percent of projected DPY.) A 1 percent shift in the saving rate would require either an offsetting decrease in personal income taxes or rise in transfer payments, or an increase of $10 billion from government purchases, to keep the economy in balance. As noted in Chapter 2, the AEI model allows the user to make his own assumption about the saving rate.

Federal Government Purchases. Federal purchases of goods and services are the only remaining demand component. Projections of federal purchases (and other NIA expenditures) under the Nixon administration and a hypothetical McGovern administration were presented in the first publication in the AEI long-range budget project series[14] and an updated version for the administration is presented in the "Options Volume." These projections give the path of federal purchases for the years 1975-80.

Total Demand and the Expenditure Gap. The projected components of demand, in 1971 dollars, are now summed to give total demand. The assumptions that have been made to obtain these projections can be summarized here:

1. Total demand is calculated for potential GNP. In particular, the income estimate on which consumption is based uses projected potential GNP.

2. Investment follows a path that holds the ratio of capital stock to potential private GNP constant.

3. Monetary policy accommodates to investment demand to permit it to follow the path just described.

4. Federal tax laws follow the path projected by the user and state and local tax receipts grow in response to GNP growth as they have in the past.

5. Government purchases follow the path projected by the user.

Total demand, estimated on the basis of these assumptions, can then be compared to potential GNP to obtain the "expenditure gap":

$$Gap = Projected\ Demand - Potential\ GNP$$

This is the excess (or deficit) of demand over projected supply, given projected tax laws and projected government spending. If the gap is positive, inflation will take place at a higher rate than the rate consistent with the chosen unemployment rate. If it is negative, unemployment will rise above the rate assumed. Thus the problem for budget policy, in this model, is to make total demand add up to potential GNP.[15]

Budget Policy to Close the Expenditure Gap

With monetary policy implicitly fixed by the investment targets discussed above, there are basically two ways to close the expenditure gap, whether it is positive or negative. These are: (a) adjustment of federal government purchases, operating directly on the demand side, or (b) a change in personal taxes or transfer payments to change PCE. (Transfer payments are the equivalent of negative taxes from the NIA point of view.) Then, once the economy is balanced at full employment, any changes in government purchases must be balanced by opposite changes in PCE through tax law changes.

The analysis began with tax revenues and transfer payments based on full-employment GNP, projected tax laws, and projected federal purchases. Any expenditure gap is then eliminated by a change in government purchases or tax revenues. Thus the resulting federal budget deficit (or surplus) is determined as the balance of projected revenue and expenditure *with zero gap*. This is the budget deficit (or surplus) that maintains the economy at full employment, given the assumptions about investment and implicit monetary policy. Thus there is nothing in the analysis that implies the necessity of a balanced full-employment budget.

Consider an increase in federal purchases beginning with a balanced economy and some given federal budget surplus (or deficit). This must be matched by a reduction in PCE to maintain constant aggregate demand equal to potential output. But if consumers only spend 90.5 cents out of each dollar of disposable income, taxes must be increased by \$1.11 (=1.00/0.905) to reduce consumer spending by \$1.00. Thus a balanced *change* in the budget —balanced in the sense that aggregate demand is unchanged—requires a larger change in transfer payments or tax revenues than the change in purchases that it finances.[16] This means that as government purchases rise in a balanced U.S. economy with investment fixed, the government surplus that balances the economy will also increase (or deficit decrease) with revenues having to rise by about \$1.11 with each \$1.00 increase in purchases.

The Long-Run Effects of Monetary Policy

Up to this point the possibility of using monetary policy to close the expenditure gap has not been raised; the discussion throughout has focused on budget policy. There are two reasons for this seeming omission. One has already been alluded to—the path of monetary policy is implicitly fixed by the assumptions concerning business investment and residential construction. In a sense, monetary policy has already been "assigned" to keeping investment on the assumed path. A second reason is that the effect of monetary policy on the *balance* of total supply and demand in the economy in the long run is not clear. A given increase in interest rates will reduce the size of the capital stock. This will have offsetting effects on demand and supply. Demand will decrease in the economy since less investment will be needed to provide growth in the capital stock as it proceeds along its new, lower growth path. But supply (potential output) will also decrease since the capital stock has been reduced. Thus the long-run effects of a given change in monetary policy on the balance of aggregate supply and demand are uncertain. In the short run, it is usually presumed that the effects on demand will exceed those on supply. But once the effects on supply begin to appear as the capital stock adjusts to the new level of interest rates, the balance swings the other way.

The relation between the long-run supply and demand effects of monetary policy can be made clearer using an example. Suppose output (Q) in the economy depends on the available stocks of capital (K) and labor (L):

$$Q = F(K,L). \tag{1.1}$$

Then a given change in interest rates (r) will effect output as follows:

$$\frac{dQ}{dr} = \frac{\delta Q}{\delta K}\frac{dK}{dr} = E(Q/K) \cdot \frac{Q}{K} \cdot \frac{dK}{dr}, \tag{1.2}$$

where $E(Q/K)$ is the elasticity of output with respect to changes in the capital stock. Equation (1.2) gives the supply effect discussed above.

On the demand side, gross investment (I), in any period, is the change in the capital stock, net investment, plus replacement investment:

$$I = \Delta K + \delta K, \tag{1.3}$$

where we assume replacement investment is a constant fraction (δ) of the capital stock. If we define the growth rate of the capital stock (g_K) as the proportional rate of change of the capital stock $(\Delta K/K)$, we have an expression for investment in terms of the capital stock:

$$I = (g_K + \delta K). \tag{1.4}$$

Then the long-run demand effect of a change in interest rates discussed above is given by:

$$\frac{dI}{dr} = (g_K + \delta)\frac{dK}{dr}. \tag{1.5}$$

Evidently, in the long run, monetary policy will have the generally expected effect on the expenditure gap—changing demand more than supply—if:

$$\frac{dI}{dr} = (g_K + \delta)\frac{dK}{dr} > E(Q/K) \cdot \frac{Q}{K}\frac{dK}{dr}. \tag{1.6}$$

Cancelling the terms dK/dr in (1.6), it can be seen that the long-run demand effect will dominate if:

$$(g_K + \delta) > E(Q/K) \cdot \frac{Q}{K}. \tag{1.7}$$

This makes the example a problem in measurement and econometrics. Thus, it is necessary to know the trend growth rate of the capital stock (g_K), the average aggregate depreciation rate (δ), the elasticity of output with respect to changes in the capital stock $(E(Q/K))$, and the ratio of output to capital. Some typical rough estimates of the values of these variables for the U.S. economy are: $g_K = 0.04$, $\delta = 0.10$, $E(Q/K) = 0.30$, $Q/K = 0.30$.[17] These values inserted into (1.7) give:

$$.04 + .10 > .30 \cdot .30 \text{ or } 0.14 > 0.09. \tag{1.7}$$

With these values of the aggregate variables in equation (1.7), the demand effect does seem to predominate. But this result is very sensitive to changes in estimated values of the key parameters. Reducing the depreciation rate to 0.8 and increasing the elasticity value to 0.4, both plausible changes, makes both sides of equation (1.7) equal to 0.12, so that a change in δ has no effect on the expenditure gap.

Thus the current state of knowledge concerning the effects of changes in monetary policy or demand and supply in the long run is not sufficiently precise that one can rule out the possibility that these effects simply cancel each other out. In the face of this uncertainty, it seems best to leave monetary policy to accommodate to the long-run investment path, and use budget policy to deal with expenditure gaps, as discussed above.

Chapter 2
THE AEI MODEL IN DETAIL

Introduction

The previous chapter provided a general framework for analyzing long-run problems of resource allocation within the U.S. economy. The purpose of this chapter is to describe and explain in detail the specific method used to render that framework operational in the AEI LRBP model.

As previously noted, the basic framework of the model outline in Chapter 1 is that of the national income and product accounts of the United States. Thus, many of the equations in the model are simply identities which come from the definitions used in constructing the accounts. For example, an equation which states that final demand on the product side is the sum of consumption demand, investment demand, government demand, and net exports, is simply an accounting identity, and will be true regardless of what values are projected for these aggregates. Equations of this type have no economic content—they imply nothing about economic behavior.

On the other hand, of necessity, some of the equations in the model *do* have economic content, and the behavior implied by these equations will only accurately reflect behavior in the real world if specific assumptions hold true. For example, it is assumed in this model that the ratio of capital to output in the economy will be constant throughout the projection period, and most of the investment equations in the model reflect this assumption. If a user of the model wishes to change this assumption, as he might, then the specific output of the model would also change. However, regardless of how one projects the components of final demand, the sum of the components would still be equal to final demand.

The purpose of this model is not to *forecast* what the economy will look like over the next ten years. Rather, its purpose is to analyze the effect of federal budget policy, given a set of assumptions about economic behavior, on key aggregates in the national income accounts, and on the balance between supply and demand in the economy as a whole. Therefore, in so far as was practicable, the model was constructed in such a way as to be useful with any set of basic economic assumptions that the user of the model might wish to choose. Thus, most of its equations are fundamentally identities, and variables which represent economic behavior are treated as parameters external to the model. Exceptions to this general procedure will be identified as they arise.

The discussion below follows closely the outline provided in Chapter 1. The first section details the calculations involved in projecting potential GNP, the GNP deflator, and the other deflators used in the model. The next section deals with the product-side components of GNP and the third section contains a discussion of the income side. The following section shows how the other parts of the model are fitted together.

The GNP Path

Potential GNP Calculations. Conceptually, calculation of potential GNP is very straightforward. One merely has to project the labor force, the unemployment rate that is consistent with "full employment," and the growth of labor productivity in the economy as a whole. Treating productivity and employment as indexes set to 1.00 in some base year, the two indexes are then multiplied together, yielding an index of real growth, and this index is then multiplied by GNP in the base year to get potential GNP defined in base-year dollars.

In practice, this procedure must be somewhat more complicated, as the NIA treat outputs of the public and private sectors differently from one another. For the private sector, the procedure outlined above may be applied straightforwardly—given estimates of private employment and private productivity—to get potential private GNP. In the public sector, on the other hand, the NIA are constructed in such a way that productivity is not permitted to change. The constant dollar output of the public sector is defined as being equal to the number of employees in general government times the average compensation per general government employee in the base year. That is, the only source of growth in real public GNP comes from increases in public employment; changes in productivity are defined to be zero for the public sector.

Thus, in projecting total annual potential GNP, annual projections are needed for the total labor force, the civilian labor force, state and local government employment, federal civilian and military employment, private employment, and private productivity. The procedures used for these calculations in the AEI model are as follows:

1. Annual projections of the total labor force (TLF), consistent with 4 percent unemployment, are given exogenously. These are then adjusted, using "Okun's Law," for the excess of the unemployment rate above 4 percent.[18]

2. The annual growth rate of private productivity (PRODR), and the annual unemployment rate in the civilian labor force (UR), and the rate of inflation in the private sector (GPGNPD), are given exogenously.[19]

3. Projections of employment in the armed forces (FEAF) (derived from the budget projection for national defense) are subtracted from TLF to get the civilian labor force (LFCIV).

4. Civilian employment (ECIV) is then calculated as (1-UR) x LFCIV.

5. Employment in the state and local government sector "tracks" off of projections of state and local purchases (explained on pp. 25-26 below). State and local purchases are projected separately for elementary and secondary education, college education and "other

functions." State and local employment in each of these areas is then obtained by multiplying the rate of growth of purchases by the 1971 level of state and local employment in each category.[26]

6. Private employment (PE) is defined as total civilian employment less state and local employment less federal government civilian employment (FECIV). The estimate of federal civilian employment used, of course, will depend upon assumptions made about federal government behavior, and is exogenous to the model.

7. Once private employment has been projected, the procedure outlined in the first paragraphs of this chapter can be straightforwardly applied to compute private GNP for each year. First, output per private worker (in 1958 dollars)[21] is computed by taking the 1971 value of this statistic (POPWRK) and increasing it at the same rate as the annual growth in private productivity.

Private GNP in 1958 dollars is simply output per worker in the private economy multiplied by private employment. State and local GNP and federal GNP are computed by multiplying the projected number of employees of each sector times the 1958 compensation per employee in the respective sector. Summing the three—private GNP, state and local GNP, and federal GNP—yields total GNP in 1958 dollars. This is then converted to GNP in 1971 dollars by multiplying by 1.416, which was the value of the GNP deflator (1958 dollars) in 1971.

In addition to a projected path for real (constant dollar) GNP, the model also requires annual values of current dollar GNP. The procedure used to compute these follows:

1. An index of productivity in the private economy (with 1971 as the base year) is computed by multiplying (for the years 1972-80) projected annual growth in productivity times the lagged value of the index:

$$\text{PRODIN}(t) = [1.0 + \text{PRODR}(t)] \times \text{PRODIN}(t-1). \tag{2.1}$$

2. Given an exogenous estimate of the annual growth of private GNP deflator (GPGNPD), the private deflator itself (in 1971 dollars) is calculated in the same manner:

$$\text{PGNPD}(t) = [1.0 + \text{GPGNPD}(t)] \times \text{PGNPD}(t-1). \tag{2.2}$$

3. Separate calculations are then made to convert private GNP into current dollars and government GNP into current dollars. The two are summed to get total GNP in current dollars. It will be recalled that in deriving the projection for total GNP in constant dollars private GNP in 1958 dollars was computed for each year. To convert this into current dollars, the 1958 dollar projections are first inflated by 1.36 (the 1971 value of the 1958 base private GNP deflator), which converts them to 1971 dollars, and then multiplied by the private GNP deflator calculated in equation (2.2). The procedure for the public sector is somewhat more complicated, as it involves making an assumption about the growth in compensation per employee in the government sector. It is assumed that compensation in the public sector will grow at the same rate as that in the private sector, since otherwise people working in government would have an incentive to leave their jobs. Private sector

compensation is assumed to increase at the rate of inflation (the private GNP deflator) plus the overall rate of growth of private productivity. Thus, it is assumed that employees in the private sector will receive, after allowing for inflation, the real value of their improved productivity. This, it may be recalled, is the standard upon which the old wage-price guide-posts were set, and also provides the underlying rationale behind the "5.5 percent rule" of the Cost of Living Council.

Current-dollar public GNP is defined, in the national income accounts, as the compensation of general government employees. Following the above argument, the annual rate of growth of compensation per worker will be the sum of the growth of private productivity and the growth of the private GNP deflator. Multiplying together the indexes of these components of increased wages (PRODIN and PGNPD, calculated in equations (2.1) and (2.2) above) yields a projection of the general government deflator, defined on a 1971 base. This projection is then multiplied by 2.028 (the 1971 value of the general government deflator on a 1958 base) and finally multiplied by the projections of government GNP in 1958 dollars that were used in calculating total GNP in 1958 dollars. The product of all this is government GNP in current dollars. This, when added to private GNP in current dollars, gives GNP in current dollars (GNPN).

Price Deflators in the AEI Model. In the NIA, the implicit price deflator for any component of GNP is defined as current dollar expenditure on that component divided by the value of that expenditure in base-year dollars. Since projections of GNP in current dollars, 1958 dollars, and 1971 dollars have already been obtained by the procedures discussed above, calculation of the implicit GNP deflator, both on a 1958 and on a 1971 base, is perfectly straightforward:

$$GNPD(t) = \frac{GNPN(t)}{GNP(t)} \,, \tag{2.3}$$

where GNP(t) is measured in constant dollars.

Calculation of implicit price deflators of the components of GNP, however, is not so straight-forward, as it involves projecting relative price changes over the next ten years. Ideally, one would like to have a good econometric model, which, allowing for supply conditions and the feedbacks of different patterns of demand onto supply, would in fact forecast such relative price changes for each set of economic and budgetary assumptions that might be used in the model. Incorporating such sophisticated features into a model of resource allocation is well beyond the scope of the current study. Therefore, except for state-local purchases, a simple ad hoc procedure, that of estimating other price deflators as linear functions of the GNP deflator, was employed. Since the national income accounts present price deflators on a 1958 base, the regressions were run for 1958 dollars and then converted into 1971 dollars by dividing the estimated values of the deflators by their respective reported 1971 values. Table 6 presents the results of the basic regressions, and the values of the standard statistical tests. These regression equations are those which are used in the model.

Table 6
ORDINARY LEAST SQUARES REGRESSIONS OF SELECTED PRODUCT-SIDE
DEFLATORS ON THE GNP DEFLATOR, 1958 = 1.00[a]
(Sample period: 1954-1971, annual data)

Implicit Deflator		Constant		Coefficient on GNP Deflator	R^2	SE[a]	DW[a]	
Personal consumption expenditure								
PCED58	=	.177 (3.13)	+	.824 (161.2)	.999	.003	.84	(2.4)
Residential investment								
RCID58	=	.154 (5.3)	+	1.172 (44.3)	.992	.016	.90	(2.5)
Producers' durable equipment								
PDED58	=	.238 (6.0)	+	.687 (16.0)	.941	.026	.31	(2.6)
Producers' structures								
PSD58	=	−.510 (10.1)	+	1.507 (33.0)	.986	.028	.78	(2.7)
Federal purchases								
FPRD58	=	−.363 (13.5)	+	1.353 (55.5)	.995	.015	1.1	(2.8)

[a]Values in parentheses are t-statistics. DW is the Durbin-Watson statistic. SE is the standard error of the estimate. As the DWs show, these are not very good structural equations. But the indicated alternative procedure, that of specifying a detailed model of GNP and relative price changes among the components of GNP, is one which the profession has been working on for years and has not yet fully implemented.

The deflator for state and local purchases is derived by assuming that (a) the employees of state and local governments will have increases in salary amounting to private productivity increases plus the increase in the private sector rate of inflation and that (b) the price of purchases made by state and local governments—other than direct compensation of employees—will increase at a rate equal to the rate of inflation implicit in the growth of the private GNP deflator.

The overall rate of price increase in each of the three categories of state and local purchases—for elementary and secondary education, college education, and other functions—is computed as a weighted sum of the assumed rate of increase for compensation per worker and the assumed rate of price increase for other purchases. About 70 percent of purchases for elementary and secondary education is for compensation of employees, leaving 30 percent for other purchases for that function. In the field of higher education, 81 percent of purchases is for direct compensation and 19 percent is for purchases of other goods.[22] Purchases used to perform the other functions of state and local government were assumed to be 44 percent direct compensation and 56 percent purchases of other goods and services.[23]

To get the deflator for state-local purchases (SPRD) in any given year, these weights are applied to the 1971 dollar projections of purchases in each category to get current dollar purchases. The 1971 dollar purchases which are direct compensation are then multiplied by both PRODIN (the index of labor productivity with a 1971 base explained above) and the private GNP deflator. Purchases which are not compensation of government employees are simply multiplied by the private GNP deflator. The current dollar projections of each component, derived in this manner, are then summed to give total state and local government purchases of goods and services in current dollars (SPRN). The state and local purchases deflator is then:[24]

$$SPRD = \frac{SPRN(t)}{SPR(t)} \qquad (2.9)$$

The Product Side

In the national income accounts, the product side is defined as simply those things which sum to gross national product. In the AEI model, GNP on the product side is separated into personal consumption expenditures (PCE), federal government purchases of goods and services for national defense (FPRDF), federal government purchases of goods and services for nondefense purposes (FPRO), state and local government purchases of goods and services (SPR), investment in producers' durable equipment (PDE), investment in producers' structures (PS), inventory investment (INVI), investment in residential structures (RCI), and net exports (NETXM). The sum of these components, by definition, is GNP, or in the context of the AEI model, final demand (FD) for GNP, in 1971 dollars.

The components of final demand are projected using specific assumptions about economic behavior. The equations that result are discussed below.

Business Investment. The assumption of a constant capital/output ratio (v) under the golden rule assumption discussed in Chapter 1 requires that the ratio of investment to output also be constant. This has been true historically, and also follows from theoretical economic models with roughly unchanging relative prices of output and investment goods.[25]

With the capital/output ratio constant we can write the gross investment function as:

$$I = K_t - K_{t-1} + \delta K_t \qquad (2.10)$$

$$= V(Q_t - Q_{t-1}) + \delta V Q_t$$

$$= V g_\phi Q_t + \delta V Q_t = V(g_\phi + \delta) Q_t \, .$$

Here g is the proportional growth rate of X and δ is the rate of depreciation of capital. Equation (2.10) just shows that holding the capital/output ratio constant implies a constant ratio of gross investment to real output $((I/Q)_t)$ as the economy grows at full employment.

Most large-scale models including the Bureau of Economic Activity (BEA) model[26] include production functions that enforce a consistency between investment and output from the supply side, that is, their investment projections give the capital stock needed to produce projected full-employment output. The BEA model projects the ratios of investment to real private GNP in 1975 and 1980 shown in Table 7.

Table 7
BEA PROJECTION OF INVESTMENT–REAL PRIVATE GNP RATIOS

Investment Category	Percent of Real Private GNP	
	1975	1980
Producers' structures	3.74	3.69
Producers' equipment	8.66	8.61
Total fixed	12.40	12.30
Inventory investment	1.54	1.09

Source: Unpublished data from Bureau of Economic Analysis, Department of Commerce.

These projections include small specific provisions for investment in antipollution devices, running to $3.6 billion (1958 dollars) in 1975 and $2.6 billion in 1980.

The BEA investment projections suggest a ratio of fixed investment to real private GNP of about 12.4 percent, and of inventories of about 1.2 percent. These ratios are also consistent with the projections given in the Council of Economic Advisers annual reports of 1970 and 1971. The ratios used in the AEI model were .012 for inventory investment, .0374 for producers' structures, and .0866 for producers' durable equipment.

Conversion of the projections of business investment in 1971 dollars to current dollars is done by multiplying the constant-dollar figures by the relevant deflators, the derivation of which was discussed above. This converts PDE to PDEN, and PS to PSN. The national income accounts do not provide an implicit deflator for inventory investment. Since inventories are, however, like the rest of GNP, subject to inflation, the implicit price deflator for private GNP was used to inflate inventory investment, yielding INVIN.

Residential Construction. Previous long-term projections of residential construction activity either (a) assumed that the requirements written into the Housing Act of 1968 are met, giving a high path of about 2.6 million starts annually, or (b) let their equations predict starts, giving a lower path of about 2.1-2.5 million starts annually.

Past data on starts, expenditures, and average price, or cost, are shown in Table 8. One remarkable thing about the data is the stable and trendless nature of the average cost numbers. This suggests that once a path for annual starts is decided on, that can simply be multiplied by $15,530—the average 1959-71 price in 1958 dollars—to obtain projected residential construction expenditures in 1958 dollars.

Table 8

HOUSING STARTS AND EXPENDITURES IN 1958 DOLLARS

Year	Expenditures in 1958 Dollars ($ in billions)	Annual Total Starts ($ in millions)	Average Cost in 1958 Dollars ($ in thousands)
1959	24.7	1.554	15.89
1960	21.9	1.296	16.89
61	21.6	1.365	15.71
62	23.8	1.492	15.91
63	24.8	1.642	15.10
64	24.2	1.561	15.46
65	23.8	1.510	15.77
66	21.3	1.196	17.89
67	20.4	1.322	15.41
68	23.2	1.545	15.01
69	23.1	1.500	15.40
1970	21.3	1.470	14.50
71	27.0	2.085	12.91

Source: *Survey of Current Business,* various issues.

For the AEI model, it seemed better to use a starts path derived from a forecast, rather than the high housing act path, which assumes a policy change. This would yield a path that seems likely in the absence of any particularly strong policy push favoring housing relative to other sectors. Then one policy option in the budget projection model would be to stimulate the residential construction sector.

A plausible full-employment 1973 level for starts might be about 2.0 million, followed by a rise of perhaps 0.1 million a year in full-employment starts. This path might flatten out when it reaches 2.4 - 2.5 million due to supply constraints and the passing of the population bulge of the early 1970s. Table 9 gives a starts path that can be multiplied by $15,530 in 1958 dollars to obtain a base RC path.

Projections of Residential Investment. In the AEI model, the average value of a new housing unit in 1958 dollars is a parameter (HC) which can take on different values for each of the years for which projections are being made. In running the model, however, the value of HC was set at $15,530 for the entire projection period. As previously noted, this was the average cost of a new unit over the period 1959 to 1971, in 1958 dollars.

House cost (HC) when multiplied by housing starts (HS) gives the 1958 dollar value of residential investment for a given year. In the AEI model, the housing starts path shown in Table 9 was used. This is then converted into 1971 dollars simply by multiplying by the

Table 9
A POSSIBLE HOUSING STARTS BASE
WITH FULL-EMPLOYMENT GROWTH

Year	Total Annual Starts (millions)
1972	2.0
73	2.1
74	2.2
75	2.3
76	2.3
77	2.4
78	2.4
79	2.5
1980	2.5

1971 value of the residential investment deflator on a 1958 base. To convert the resulting 1971 dollar series (RCI) to current dollars (RCIN), the residential investment deflator described above is used.

Government Purchases of Goods and Services. Federal purchases of goods and services are exogenous to the model, that is, they are an input from the budget projections. As the model is structured, federal purchases of goods and services must be given in constant 1971 dollars on an NIA basis. (Other components of the federal budget must also be given on an NIA basis, but in current dollars.)[27] Given current-dollar federal purchases from the budget projection, the federal purchases deflator, whose derivation is described above, is used to convert federal purchases in 1971 dollars to federal purchases in current dollars (FPRN).

State and local purchases are calculated on the assumption that population growth will follow Census Series E,[28] school and college enrollment will follow the path given in Census Series E-1,[29] and that the increase in the overall quality of state and local government services will take place at the same average annual rate as it did for the period 1954-1971. Given this information, state and local government purchases (in 1971 dollars) are projected separately for elementary and secondary education, college education, and "other functions," by means of the following general procedure:[30]

$$SP(f,t) = [SP(f,1971)/POP(f,1971)] \times SQR(f)(t-1) \times POP(f,t), \quad (2.11)$$

where SP is state and local purchases (NIA basis), POP is population, SQR is 1 plus the average annual rate of increase of scope and quality from 1954-71, the subscript f represents the category of purchases (e.g., elementary and secondary education) and t represents the year, with 1971 equal to 1. Thus equation (2.11) says that for any of the three functional categories of expenditure for which projections were made, state and local purchases (in 1971 dollars) would equal 1971 purchases per person in the relevant population, times an index of increased scope and quality, times the relevant population in the year for which the projection is made.[31]

With the constant dollar amounts for state and local purchases of goods and services calculated as shown in equation (2.11), projected spending for the three categories is summed to get total state and local purchases in constant dollars. Projected state and local government employment is then derived by multiplying the growth in purchases in each category $(SP(f,t)/SP(f,1971))$, times the 1971 level of state and local government employment in each category.[32]

The resulting projections of total purchases and employment can be considered baseline projections. That is, if users of the model are interested in the effect of policies which would alter the amount of resources used by state and local governments, these projections should be revised. For this reason, the model contains two exogenous variables which can be used to add to or subtract from the baseline projection of purchases and employment. The two variables are called SPRAO—state and local purchases (add-on) defined in 1971 dollars—and SEAO—state and local employment (add-on). The final projection of state and local general government employment and purchases calculated by the model consists of the baseline projections discussed above plus the "add-ons," SPRAO and SEAO.

Current-dollar state and local purchases (SPRN) are obtained by multiplying state and local purchases in 1971 dollars by the deflator for this type of spending (SPRD).

Net Exports. Net exports are very difficult to estimate, given the current uncertainty about the future context in which international trade and finance will be conducted. Here, they were assumed to be zero in each year, although the model is capable of easily accepting revisions in that assumption. As currently programmed, it accepts as exogenous data series for exports and imports in 1971 dollars. Furthermore, import and export deflators are generated, so that the 1971 dollar projections can be converted into current dollars. In the past, however, net exports have not constituted a very significant part of GNP. To the extent that they are part of GNP, their omission will tend to understate final demand, and hence the excess of claims over resources, generated by the model. While this is unfortunate, there did not seem any practical way to project net exports any more accurately than to assume that they will be zero.

Consumption. Consumption (PCE) in the AEI model, provides the link between the income and the product side. PCE in real terms is determined by first multiplying disposable personal income (DPY) by a ratio of PCE to DPY (the consumption ratio) and then deflating the result by the PCE deflator (PCED). This procedure basically divides DPY into three fractions—personal income plus transfers to foreigners (PIT), PCE, and personal saving (PS). These fractions are held constant during the projection period.

Table 10 shows the disposition of DPY among its three components for the period 1960 through the third quarter of 1972. The columns give totals in billions of dollars and fractions of DPY. Since all components will be deflated by the PCE deflator, the ratios are the same in current and constant dollars.

The first thing to notice about the data is the stability of the PIT ratio at 2.5 percent of DPI since 1965. Given this stability, the PIT ratio can be put with reasonable confidence at 2.5 percent, and attention be centered on the division of the remaining 97.5 percent of DPY between PCE and PS.

The PCE and PS ratios show clearly the recent rise in the saving ratio and drop in the consumption ratio. This is well known. However, a closer inspection of the saving ratio since 1963 suggests the possibility of a rising trend in the saving ratio. Even discounting the 4.9 figure for 1963, the saving ratio seems to have risen fairly steadily since the early 1960s, interrupted only by the surtax years of 1968 and 1969. In those years the saving ratio fell as people paid the surtax mainly by reducing saving, rather than cutting consumption. One estimate by Branson suggests that the surtax (2 percent of personal income) was paid two-thirds out of saving and one-third out of consumption.[33] This means that in the full surtax year 1969, the saving rate would have been 1.2 (2/3 x 2.0) higher in the absence of the surcharge. This would have meant a saving rate of 7.2 or 7.3 percent in 1969, reasonably in line with the upward trend since the early 1960s.

Table 10
DISPOSITION OF DISPOSABLE INCOME AMONG ITS COMPONENTS
(1960 − 1972)

Year	Disposable Personal Income ($ in billions)	Personal Consumption Expenditure ($ in billions)	(percent)	Personal Interest Plus Foreign Transfers ($ in billions)	(percent)	Personal Savings ($ in billions)	(percent)
1960	350.0	325.2	92.9	7.8	2.2	17.0	4.9
61	364.4	335.2	92.0	8.1	2.2	21.2	5.8
62	385.3	355.1	92.2	8.6	2.2	21.6	5.6
63	404.6	375.0	92.7	9.7	2.4	19.9	4.9
64	438.1	401.2	91.6	10.7	2.4	26.2	6.0
65	473.2	432.8	91.5	12.0	2.5	28.4	6.0
66	511.9	466.3	91.1	13.0	2.5	32.5	6.4
67	546.3	492.1	90.1	13.9	2.5	40.4	7.4
68	591.0	536.2	90.8	15.0	2.5	39.8	6.7
69	634.2	579.6	91.4	16.7	2.6	37.9	6.0
1970	689.5	616.8	89.6	16.9	2.5	54.9	8.0
71	744.4	664.9	89.3	17.6	2.4	60.9	8.2
72	795.1	721.0	90.6	19.2	2.4	54.8	6.9

Source: *Survey of Current Business,* various issues.

The consequence of these movements in the saving rate, given the stable PIT ratio, is the drop in the consumption fraction from levels around 92.5 percent in the early 1960s to 90 percent in 1967 and on down to around 89.3 percent in 1970-71, interrupted by a small increase in the surtax years.

On the other hand, it can also be argued that the rise in the savings ratio coincided with the accelerating inflation of 1966-71, and that the slowdown in the inflation rate in 1971 and 1972 is producing a reversal of the saving ratio to levels more in line with long-run experience. Beginning in the third quarter of 1971, the personal saving ratio fell from the peak of 8.6 percent in the second quarter of 1971 to 6.4 percent in the third quarter of 1972.

The data thus can be interpreted to suggest a rising trend in the saving ratio, or the rise can be discounted as the result of unanticipated inflation in the last years of the 1960s. Thus a serious problem is presented in projecting the saving ratio into the future. The seriousness of the problem can be clearly seen by looking ahead to 1975. Projected DPY in 1975 is about $1 trillion. Moving from the Council of Economic Advisers[34] assumption of a 6.5 percent saving ratio (a 91.0 percent consumption ratio) to 8.0 percent on saving (89.5 percent on consumption) shifts 1.5 percent—$15 billion—from consumer demand to saving at that level of DPY. This essentially frees $15 billion in output to be absorbed elsewhere—by federal spending, for instance—with no increase in the excess of demand over potential output in the economy. Thus while the council projections might include a full-employment surplus of $12 billion in 1975 to maintain supply and demand balance in the economy, moving to an 8.0 percent saving rate would mean that a deficit of $3 billion would be needed, holding all other elements of the projections unchanged. The basic problem is that a 1 percent variation in the saving rate is small by statistical standards—perhaps insignificant—but large from the point of view of budget projections.

The AEI model allows the user to select his own saving rate projections. In the "Options Volume,"[35] this rate was set at 7 percent, somewhat above the experience of 1960-66, but considerably below the ratios observed during 1967-71. Since, given the PS ratio, PCE depends on disposable personal income, the discussion in the next section details the derivation of DPY from GNP in the AEI model.

The Income Side

The income-side calculations in the AEI model serve many purposes. The overall model of resource allocation described in Chapter 1 requires that an estimate of personal consumption be derived from the income side. That is, personal consumption is assumed to be a function of personal income, and not (directly) of GNP. On the other hand, the other product-side variables are viewed within the model as being directly related to GNP, or in the case of housing, as growing on trend in the absence of explicit government policies designed to stimulate (or retard) that growth. In addition, a number of income-side variables (such as corporate profits) are necessary for projecting federal, state and local government budgets, a major purpose of the AEI LRBP.[36]

The procedure used for projecting personal income, given a current-dollar GNP path, involves the derivation of personal income and is essentially the same as that used in Table 1.9 of any July issue of the *Survey of Current Business*. (See also Table 3 above.) This requires that projections be obtained for capital consumption allowance (corporate, CCCA, and non-corporate, NCCCA), indirect business taxes and nontaxes (both federal, FIBT, and state and local, SIBT), statistical discrepancy (assumed to be zero), subsidies less current surpluses of government enterprises (both federal, FSUBLS, and state and local, SSURPE), corporate profits and inventory valuation adjustment, contributions for social insurance (federal, FCSI, state and local, SCSI), wage accruals less disbursements (assumed to be zero), government transfers to persons (federal, FTRF, state and local, STRF), interest (net) paid by government and consumers (federal, FINT, state and local, SINT, and personal, PINT), and dividends (DIV). Disposable personal income (DPY) is then derived by subtracting personal taxes and nontaxes from personal income.

While the procedure of estimating these income-side variables and subtracting them from nominal GNP is conceptually straightforward, practical application of the procedure is complicated by the fact that many of the income-side variables—notably taxes and transfers—themselves depend on the estimate of personal income. The procedure used in the AEI model was to first calculate all the variables that are assumed to depend only on GNP, and then to project the remaining variables, as well as DPY and its uses, by an iterative process. The remainder of this section will deal with the straightforward part of the procedure and then with the iterative technique that was used to get the end result—projections of DPY and the disposition of DPY.

Noncorporate capital consumption allowances (NCCCA) were projected using an equation which was estimated by means of ordinary least squares from annual data from 1954 through 1971. The equation is:

$$NCCCA(t) = 1.19 + .09696\ GNPN(t) + .6995\ NCCCA(t-1), \qquad (2.12)$$
$$(3.2)\quad (4.5) \qquad\qquad (8.5)$$

$$R^2 = .999$$
$$SE = .193$$
$$DW = 1.98$$

Net corporate cash flow (CCF)—gross corporate profits, corporate capital consumption allowances, and corporate inventory valuation adjustments—was assumed to be a constant fraction of nominal GNP consistent with the assumption about steady-state growth discussed in Chapter 1.[37] The fraction of GNP used in the model (CFR) is 16 percent. This is consistent with recent experience at times of full employment (1955, 1965, and 1966).

Federal contributions for social insurance are exogenous to the model, as these are among the policy variables that the model was designed to study. State and local CSI which, for the most part, is made up of contributions to state and local government pension funds, is assumed to maintain its current ratio to current dollar state and local purchases: 6.8 percent.

The current surplus of state and local government enterprises (SSURPE) is assumed to grow, from its 1971 level, at the rate of growth of nominal GNP. Federal subsidies less current surplus of government enterprises (FSUBLS) are exogenous, with the largest portions coming from separate budget projections of housing subsidies, the postal service, and the Commodity Credit Corporation, with the remainder assumed to follow its recent trend value of approximately zero. The algebraic sum of SSURPE and FSUBLS yields the total subsidies less current surplus of government enterprise (SUBLS).

Dividends are projected by an equation estimated by ordinary least squares, using annual data from 1954 to 1971:

$$DIV(t) = .07925 \ CCF(t) + .599 \ DIV(t-1), \qquad\qquad (2.13)$$
$$\quad\;\;\; (4.7) \qquad\qquad (6.6)$$

$$R^2 = .995$$
$$SE = .389$$
$$DW = 1.87$$

State and local transfers to persons for purposes other than that of public assistance (STRFO) are assumed to be equal to 69 percent of state and local contributions for social insurance. This has been roughly true in the past, and there was no simple econometric relationship that seemed to do any better than this rough rule in predicting STRFO. State and local transfers for public assistance (STRFRA) are exogenous to the model, as these are greatly affected by federal government policy. Total state and local transfers (STRF) are simply the sum of STRFO and STRFPA.

Federal government transfers to persons (FTRF), a policy variable, are calculated by subtracting projected federal transfers to foreigners (FFA) from the exogenously given path for total federal transfers (OASDI). FFA is assumed to grow, from 1971 level, at the same rate as nominal GNP. Total transfers to persons (TRF) are equal to federal transfers to persons plus total state and local transfers.

To be consistent with the assumption of a constant capital/output ratio, state and local property taxes (SPT) are together assumed to be a constant fraction of GNP, holding their 1971 fraction of 3.8 percent.

Net interest paid by the federal government (FINT) and net interest paid by state and local governments (SINT) are both exogenous to the model. The estimates for the former were derived from budget projections of the LRBP project. The latter was assumed to maintain its current (1971) value of 0.4 billion dollars per year.

State and local personal taxes and nontaxes are assumed, in the model, to have an elasticity with respect to GNP of 1.7. The fact that this elasticity is considerably higher than unity reflects both progressivity in personal income taxes and anticipated increases in personal tax rates. This estimate has been used in a number of recent studies of state and local finance.[38]

All of the above variables in the AEI LRBP model can be projected by using information already generated within the model, or in the case of the exogenous variables, using information from outside the model. In order to project disposable personal income, however, projections of federal personal taxes and nontaxes, and of indirect business taxes other than state and local property taxes, are required. These variables, in turn, are dependent on projections of taxable personal income (personal income plus employee contributions for social insurance) and personal consumption expenditure.

Personal contributions for social insurance are assumed to maintain their 1971 share of 48.6 percent of total CSI. The estimate for federal personal tax and nontax receipts is given by equations (2.14) through (2.17). First, personal tax liability (TPSOI) is estimated as follows:[39]

$$TPSOI^*(t) = -.936(t) + (.193)(.868)[YPT(t) - YPT(0)] + TPSOI^*(0), \qquad (2.14)$$

where:

$TPSOI^*(t)$ = tax liability in year (t), assuming no changes in the tax law (1966 law applies);

t = year (1969 = 1);

$YPT(t)$ = personal taxable income in any year t (= personal income—transfer payments + personal contributions for social insurance);

$YPT(0)$ = personal taxable income at the beginning of the period (1968);

$TPSOI^*(0)$ = tax liability at the beginning of the period (1968), without the tax surcharge.

To reflect tax law changes instituted after 1966, a multiplicative factor (TS) was computed using the 1966 Treasury Department tax file.[40] Thus, for any year t:

$$TPSOI(t) = TPSOI^*(t) \, TS(t) \qquad (2.15)$$

The value of TS computed for each year where a change in the tax law took place is given by:

$$TS_{68} = 1.075$$
$$TS_{69} = 1.100$$
$$TS_{70} = 1.01$$
$$TS_{71} = .93$$
$$TS_{72} = .93$$

For 1973 and after, TS_{72} is used, thus assuming no further changes in the present tax law.

Converting tax liability to NIA tax and nontax receipts, and allowing for an "add-on" variable (CTP), the following relationship was used in the model:

$$FTPNIA(t) = TPSOI(t) + (\Delta FS(t) + NT(t) + B(t)) + CTP(t), \qquad (2.16)$$

where:

$\Delta FS(t)$ = change in final settlement in year t;

$NT(t)$ = gift and estate tax receipts and nontax receipts received in year t;

$B(t)$ = back taxes received in year t.

The value of $(\Delta FS(t) + NT(t) + B(t))$ was determined by observing the relation between personal tax liability and receipts and applying an adjustment factor, C_2, equal to 0.05 of tax liability. Thus, equation (2.15) may be written as:

$$FTPNIA(t) = TPSOI(t)(1 + C_2) + CTP(t) \qquad (2.17)$$

Indirect business taxes other than property taxes are, for the most part, sales taxes of one sort or another. As such, assuming that rates do not change, and the pattern of consumption among commodities taxed at different rates holds roughly constant, these should maintain a constant share of personal consumption expenditure. The ratios used (FIBTR for federal, SIBTR for state and local) were, respectively, .028 and .062. These were the ratios which obtained in the most recent available data: the first and second quarters of 1972 for the federal ratio, and the year 1971 for the state and local data.[41]

As was pointed out above, these equations depend on each other. Personal taxable income (and, therefore, personal taxes) in part depend upon indirect business taxes, which are subtracted from GNP in deriving YPT. Indirect business taxes, on the other hand, are assumed to depend on consumption, which cannot be known until disposable personal income, which depends on personal income taxes, has been projected.

The method employed to deal with the problem of projecting a number of variables which depend on each other is iteration. In the case at hand, the procedure is as follows:

1. A projected value for personal income less net personal interest payments less transfer payments plus indirect business taxes other than property taxes is obtained by subtracting the projected values of noncorporate capital consumption allowances, corporate cash flow including IVA, contributions for social insurance, and state and local property taxes from the projected value of nominal GNP, and then adding the projected values of net interest paid by governments, dividend payments, and total government subsidies less current surpluses of government enterprises.

2. A projected value of taxable personal income (YPT) is then obtained by adding employee contributions for social insurance (PCSI) and a "trial value" for net interest paid by consumers (PINT) to the number obtained under (1) above, and then subtracting a "trial value" for indirect business taxes other than property taxes. The trial values are obtained by assuming that the shares of these two variables in nominal GNP will, to a first approximation, be constant from year to year.

3. The resulting first estimate of YPT is then used in the personal tax equations discussed above.

4. Once personal taxes have been calculated, a first projected value for disposable personal income is obtained by adding transfer payments to the projected value of YPT,

subtracting both federal, state, and local personal taxes and nontaxes, and subtracting PCSI.

5.   Disposable personal income is then divided up into consumption, saving, personal interest paid (net), and personal transfers to foreigners, using the ratios discussed earlier.

6.   Once estimates of these variables have been obtained, the model returns to step one (above), using the calculated values instead of the old trial values. This process is continued until two successive estimates of DPY differ by one-tenth of 1 percent.[42] At that point, the final projected values are calculated, and it is these values that are used in the remaining calculations and the final output of the model.

Final Output

Having obtained a projected path for current dollar personal consumption from the income side, PCEN is deflated by the PCE deflator and added to the other product-side variables—defined in 1971 dollars—to get final demand (FD). Final demand is then subtracted from GNP, in 1971 dollars, to get the GAP, or the excess of demand over supply. (If the GAP is negative, of course, an excess of supply is implied.) The current-dollar GAP (GAPN) is calculated by multiplying the constant-dollar GAP by the GNP deflator, the derivation of which was explained above.

It should be stressed that the GAPs produced at this point are computed under the assumption that any projected state and local government surpluses or deficits will be realized. Since, in the past, the state and local sector has always been in an approximate balance, this assumption may not be a very good one. To the extent that projected surpluses are not realized, the GAP that is calculated by the model will be too low, as the surpluses will in fact add to demands on GNP, either directly through state and local government purchases, or indirectly, via consumption, through tax relief. To the extent that any projected deficits are not realized, the calculated GAP will be too high. The user of the model should be aware of this problem, and may want to modify his interpretation of the GAP as calculated according to his own opinion of what, in fact, will happen to any projection of surplus or deficit in the state and local government sector of the national income accounts.[43]

It would be a coincidence if the current-dollar product side, derived by applying the relevant price deflators to each of the constant (1971) dollar product-side components and then summing them, was just equal in value to the current dollar product side derived by inflating final demand directly by the GNP deflator. In the national income accounts, these two methods of converting real GNP into nominal GNP do in fact always yield the same result, because the overall GNP deflator is defined by the procedure of adding up the deflated components on the product side.

However, in the AEI model where the overall GNP deflator is derived from an exogenous assumption about the rate of growth of prices in the private sector and the effect of this on wage inflation in the public sector, there is no reason for the two methods of calculating nominal GNP to yield the same answer, and indeed, they do not. Thus, in order to preserve the consistency of the accounts in the model it is necessary to "force" the two measures of nominal GNP to be equal.

This was accomplished by computing the variable DEFERR (the deflator sum), equal to demand derived by adding the individually inflated components divided into the value obtained by inflating total final demand by the GNP deflator. DEFERR thus represents the excess of the overall GNP deflator over the GNP deflator implicit in the component deflators as calculated. A value of unity for DEFERR means that the two methods of computing final demand yield identical results (as they should). A value of 1.01 would indicate that nominal GNP in the aggregate has been projected as being 1 percent larger than nominal GNP as the sum of its components. In order to assure an *ex ante* value of 1.0 for DEFERR, the calculated value of DEFERR, in each year, is multiplied, in turn, times each variable that is defined in current dollars. Thus, if DEFERR is 1.01 for a given year, each component of GNP, as well as all of the income-side components, is increased by 1 percent, thus ensuring that the projected value of nominal GNP in the aggregate will be the same as the sum of the projected values of its components.[44]

The model at this point also calculates the change in personal taxes necessary to balance the economy (NPTN) and the rate of value added tax (consumption type) required to eliminate the gap (VATR). The formula for the tax increase necessary to change consumption by the amount of the gap (in current dollars) is:

$$NPTN(t) = GAPN \times \left\{ 1.0 + [FIBTR + SIBTR] \times APC \right\} / APC , \qquad (2.18)$$

where APC is the fraction of DPY that is consumed and FIBTR + SIBTR is the fraction of consumption that goes to indirect business taxes other than property taxes.

In producing the income and product projections discussed in the pages above, the AEI model projects all of the variables necessary to projecting federal and state and local budgets, on a NIA basis, except for corporate profits tax accruals. State and local corporate profits tax accruals, which have not been large in the past, are assumed to have an elasticity with respect to nominal GNP of 1.2. This is consistent with the estimates used in the studies of state and local finance referred to in the discussion of the state and local personal income tax.

Federal corporate profits tax accruals are projected by means of a corporation income tax function which is conceptually simple. It relates tax liability to corporate profits and the rate structure:

$$FCT(t) = TRC(t)CP(t) - h(t)CPDE(t) , \qquad (2.19)$$

where:

FCT(t)   = corporate tax accruals in year t;

TRC(t)   = effective tax rate on corporate profits in year t;
         $= \dfrac{\text{corporate taxes before investment tax credit}}{\text{corporate profits before tax}}$;

CP(t)   = corporate profits before taxes in year t;

h   = average corporate investment tax credit rate, i.e., loss of corporate tax revenue from investment credit divided by corporate investment in producers' durable equipment CPDE;

CPDE   = corporate investment in equipment qualifying for the credit, where C is the ratio of corporate PDE to total PDE.

This equation requires an annual projection of corporate profits themselves, which is derived as follows:

1.   Corporate capital consumption allowances are assumed, in the absence of changes in depreciation guidelines, to be a constant fraction of total corporate cash flow (CCF), the derivation of which was described above. This fraction (CCCAR) was set in the AEI model at .356, the ratio of corporate capital consumption allowances to net cash flow in 1968. In addition, an adjustment factor for changes in depreciation guidelines (DEPA) is incorporated into the equation for projecting corporate capital consumption allowances as follows:

$$CCCA(t) = CCF(t) \times (CCCAR + DEPA(t)) . \qquad (2.20)$$

Thus, the effective ratio of CCCA to CCF can be raised by means of DEPA for any projection year to account for changes in depreciation guidelines. For the AEI projections, the most important of these is the effect of the ADR system of accelerated depreciation on profits subject to tax. Estimates of the effect of ADR on corporate profits have been made by the Treasury and the Commerce departments.[45] For 1975, these estimates indicate that corporate profits subject to tax will be reduced by $6.9 billion due to the ADR system. The AEI model generates about $230 billion of corporate cash flow in 1975, of which $81 billion (35.2 percent) is capital consumption allowances. Thus, DEPA is set at .0293 to raise CCA (lower corporate profits) by $7 billion. That is, DEPA is computed as the percent of corporate cash flow (plus IVA) of the change in corporate profits due to ADR, or any other tax provision having this effect.

2.   Corporate inventory valuation adjustments (CIVA) are assumed to grow at the same rate as nominal GNP from a 1971 base.

3. Corporate profits themselves are calculated as cash flow minus corporate capital consumption allowances minus corporate inventory valuation adjustment. This is simply an identity from the national income accounts, and provides the necessary projections of corporate profits so that the equation for corporate profits tax accruals (given above) can be employed.

4. Somewhat involved outside calculations are needed to derive the appropriate average effective corporate tax rate (TCR). Starting with corporate profits before taxes (before inventory valuation adjustment), the following calculations are made for each calendar year to derive TRC (1975 figures are used to illustrate the calculation):

Item		Amount ($ in billions)
1. Corporate profits before taxes[a]		147.6
2. Adjustments to obtain tax base		−6.7
a. Federal reserve bank profits[b]	−3.6	
b. Rest of world profits[b]	−7.4	
c. SBC profits[b]	−3.4	
d. Deficits[b]	13.7	
e. State corporate income taxes[a]	−6.0	
3. Base for federal tax		140.9
4. Gross federal tax (.42[b] times line 3 above)		59.2
5. Adjustments to gross tax		−9.3
a. Foreign tax credit[b]	−6.7	
b. Investment tax credit[b]	−4.7	
c. Effects of Revenue Act of 1969[b]	1.4	
d. DISC[b]	−0.3	
e. Refunds[b]	1.0	
6. Tax liability of private corporations		49.9
7. Federal corporate tax, NIA (line 6 + line 2a)		53.5
8. Tax before investment tax credit (line 7 − line 5b)		58.2
9. TRC (line 8 / line 1)		.394

[a] Obtained from model as explained in text.

[b] Unpublished Treasury Department estimates.

All of the information necessary to project the product side, income side, and government budgets is obtained by use of the procedures described up to this point. The remainder of the model consists of a number of equations which organize the data in ways which may be useful to the user. (For example, the various categories of federal expenditure are added to get a total, annual growth rates of personal consumption are computed, et cetera.)

The next chapter presents all the output generated by the model, following a "user guide" which describes how to operate the model after it is stored in a computer.

Chapter 3
MODEL USER'S GUIDE AND THE AEI BUDGET PROJECTION RUN

This chapter presents a detailed description of how the AEI LRBP model is programmed and set up for running. The first section is a "user's guide" to the model. The next section presents the actual run done for the initial volume in this LRBP series. In the following section, problems of using the model on systems other than the PDP-10 used here are considered. (A source listing of the computer program for the AEI LRBP model is contained in Appendix B.)

A User's Guide to the AEI Model

The AEI model program was originally designed for use on a DEC-10 time sharing system. Hence, the user's guide which follows is oriented towards "conversational usage" of the program rather than "batch" usage.

Conversational usage of the AEI model requires that the user enter the appropriate information to each request for data. A request for data may be made by either the computer system or the AEI model. Requests made by the computer system will usually be indicated with a period (.). Requests made by the AEI model will be preceded by a user-oriented message describing the type of data to be entered.

In the documentation that follows, each user-oriented message appears in capital letters *without* underlining, while each response entered by the user appears in capital letters *with* underlining. Each user response must be appropriately terminated by depressing the carriage return key, and the symbol [CR] will denote that this operation is to be performed. In addition, correct spacing is critical for certain user responses. When this occurs, the symbol △ will be employed to indicate that "one space is required"; otherwise spacing may be as desired.

The operational procedures that follow are grouped into three categories: (A) Gaining access to the computer system, (B) running the AEI model, and (C) leaving the computer system. In categories (A) and (C), all the user responses are to requests for data by the computer system, while category (B) consists of user responses to requests made by the AEI model program.

Gaining Access to the Computer System.[46] The following steps are performed to gain access to the computer system:

1. If the terminal is not operating, turn the power switch to "on."

2. Telephone the computer system that will be used in running the AEI model.

3. When a continuous tone is heard in the receiver, place the receiver firmly in the acoustic coupler.

4. When the computer system properly connects with the terminal, an indicator lamp will light to denote that this step is complete.

5. The computer system will now respond with:

PLEASE LOGIN OR ATTACH

6. Following the period (.), the user should type the word LOGIN, followed by a space, and the account number assigned to him by his computer representative. A correct response would be:

LOGIN △ 2327,506 [CR]

7. The computer will process the entry and if valid respond with:

PASSWORD:

The user should respond by typing the password assigned to him by his computer representative and depressing the carriage return key [CR]. The user's response will not print on the terminal sheet. If the password is valid, the computer system will respond with a message such as this:

0900   24   MAR   73   SAT

8. At this point, the user has gained access to the system and may begin execution of the AEI model by entering:

.RUN △ MODEL [CR]

Running the AEI Model. At this point, execution of the AEI model has begun and results in the following messages:

LRBP MODEL VERSION OF 03/24/73
FAMILIAR WITH PROG? (OK OR NO)

The last message above asks the user if he is familiar with the operation of the program. The correct user response is one of the two codes enclosed by the parenthesis.[47] From this point on, the AEI model will make various requests for data with each request being preceded by a message. Each message consists of a step number, an abbreviated description of the data requested and an extended description of the data requested. By responding with NO, the user indicates that he wants all three segments of the message printed. On the other hand, a response of OK[48] indicates that the user is experienced with the procedural steps that follow and, therefore, does not require the third segment of each message, i.e., the extended description of the data requested. By employing this option, communications made by the AEI model to the user are reduced to an abbreviated form, thereby decreasing processing time. One correct response would be:

NO[CR]

The program would then print the following message:

1. DATE   ENTER AS (99/99/99)

The user responds by entering the current data as illustrated below:

03/24/73[CR]

Following the user's entry, the program asks:

DATA OK? (OK OR NO)

After each data entry by the user, the program will request verification that the data was entered correctly. If the user responds with NO, the program will repeat the previous data request; in this case step 1. A user response of OK instructs the program to continue with the next step. One correct entry would be:

OK[CR]

(Note: When multiple runs are performed, this step will occur on the first run only and any additional runs will begin at step 2.)

The next message from the program appears as:

2. TITLE   ENTER UP TO 48 CHARACTERS

The user would respond to this request with some title not exceeding forty-eight characters in length, including spaces. This title will appear at the top of each page of the output along with the date from step 1. The user would enter a title such as:

Following the entry of the title, the program requests data verification with the following message:

DATA OK? (OK OR NO)

If the user responds with NO, step 2 will be repeated; otherwise a response of OK instructs the program to continue with the next step. One appropriate response follows:

OK[CR]

The next data request message made by the program is:

3. PARAM   LIST AND/OR CHANGE (LO, CO, LC, OR NO)

At this point, the user has reached the first of two major data input sections. In order to ensure maximum flexibility of the economic assumptions, most of the equations in the model are constructed so that the specific values assigned to coefficients of the predetermined variables can be changed in this step.[49] The first successful run of the model will preset each parameter with a "programmed" initial value given in this document. If the user replaces the "programmed" initial value of a parameter with one of his own, then the "user's" initial value will be maintained on all subsequent runs. Hence, the above message requests that the user direct the program to perform one of four operations on the parameters of the model's equations. The user should respond with one of the four operation codes enclosed in the parenthesis. The operations represented by the codes are as follows:

LO (List Only). This code instructs the program to produce a listing of all the preset values assigned to each parameter variable. Upon completion of the list, the program repeats this step. LO should be employed when the user is uncertain of the value assigned to a parameter and desires to check on it.

CO (Change Only). This code instructs the program to print a data request message and prepare to accept the "user's" initial values. CO should be employed when the user is certain of the changes he will make.

LC (List and Change). This code instructs the program to produce a listing of all the preset values assigned to each parameter variable. Upon completion of the list, the program prints a data request message and prepares to accept the "user's" initial values. LC should be employed when the user is making multiple runs and does not remember if he changed a preset value on the previous run but is certain that he will change some preset value on the current run.

NO (No changes or list). This code instructs the program to maintain the current preset values and continue with the next step.

40

One of the responses the user could choose would be:

CO[CR]

The program would then reply with the data request message below:

DATA   (SPACE$PARAM VN1=9.9, VN2=9.9, $)

Following the above message, the program is ready to accept the "user's" initial values for *one or more* of the parameters. In entering the data, each parameter whose value is to be changed must be identified by a variable name (VN) that the program recognizes. Table 11 contains a complete list of the variable names assigned to each parameter, its economic name, a description of its function in the model and its "programmed" initial value. Immediately following each variable name that is entered as data, there must appear an equals sign, the user's initial value, and a comma. As an illustration, suppose that the user desires the following changes:

Economic Name and Description	Variable Name	"Programmed" Initial Value	User's Initial Value
Ratio of federal indirect business taxes to personal consumption expenditures	FIBTR	0.028	0.035
The savings rate as a fraction of disposable personal income	S	0.07	0.09
Tax adjustment parameter, federal personal income tax, 1972 value	TS	0.93	0.90
Depreciation adjustment, 1973 value	DEPA	0.0238	0.0242

To accomplish this, the user could respond with:

Δ$PARAMΔ FIBTR=0.035, S=0.09, TS(2)=0.90, DEPA(3)=0.0242, $[CR]

Table 11
VARIABLE NAME, ECONOMIC NAME, DESCRIPTION, AND PROGRAMMED INITIAL VALUES FOR THE PARAMETERS OF THE MODEL

Variable Name	Economic Name and Description	Programmed Initial Value
CCCAR	The ratio of corporate capital consumption allowances to corporate cash flow plus corporate IVA. Since the model assumes that the Golden Rule is obtained, cash flow plus corporate IVA is a constant fraction of GNP. Thus, this parameter divides cash flow into CCA and profits net of IVA. Allowance has been made to adjust this fraction (through DEPA below) for yearly changes in depreciation laws.	0.356
CFR	The ratio of corporate cash flow plus corporate IVA to GNP. The use of a simple ratio here follows from the assumption of a constant capital/output ratio.	0.160
CIVA71	Corporate inventory valuation adjustment in 1971. This is employed in the corporate IVA equation to provide for a constant rate of growth in corporate IVA.	−4.70
COLER	The percentage of real purchases in public higher education that is spent for direct compensation of employers.	0.81
EDIT	This is a technical parameter which provides the user the option of monitoring the behavior of the iterative block of the model. If EDIT=0, the option is declined. If EDIT=1, the program prints each step of the iterative block.	0
EPS	This is a technical parameter employed in the iterative block of the model. It defines the value of ΔDPY/DPY which terminates iteration.	0.001
FIBTR	The ratio of federal indirect business taxes to personal consumption expenditures.	0.028
ITERL	This is the iteration limit on the iterative block of the model.	10
PIR	The ratio of personal interest payments to disposable personal income.	0.025

Variable Name	Economic Name and Description	Programmed Initial Value
S	The savings rate as a fraction of disposable personal income.	0.07
SIBTR	The ratio of state and local indirect business taxes (excluding property taxes) to personal consumption expenditures.	0.062
SPTR	The ratio of state and local property taxes to GNP.	0.038
TNIA	An adjustment factor for converting SOI personal tax receipts (federal) to an NIA basis; i.e., TPNIA = TPSOI x (1.0 + TNIA)	0.050

(Table 11 continued on next page.)

Table 11 – Continued

Variable Name	Economic Name and Description	Programmed Initial Value									
		1 71	2 72	3 73	4 74	5 75	6 76	7 77	8 78	9 79	10 80
CTP(*)	Add-on to federal personal taxes and nontax receipts (used for private school credits and other purposes).	0.0	0.0	0.0	0.0	−0.4	−0.4	−0.4	−0.4	−0.4	−0.4
DEPA(*)	An adjustment factor to allow for the effect of changes in depreciation laws on the split between profits and CCA. The equation is written as: Corp. CCA = (Corp. CF + Corp. IVA) x (CCCAR + DEPA)	.0100	.0180	.0238	.0259	.0293	.0293	.0254	.0220	.0199	.0179
ITC(*)	This is an adjustment for the effect of an investment tax credit on federal corporate tax accruals. If the tax credit is in effect, the value of ITC should be set equal to 1; otherwise, it should be set equal to 0.	1	1	1	1	1	1	1	1	1	1
SPRB(*)	1971 calendar year purchases of goods and services by state and local governments.	135.4	0.0	0.0	0.0	0.0	0.0	0.0	0.0	0.0	0.0
TRC(*)	The effective rate of federal taxation on corporate profits.	.424	.410	.400	.415	.394	.394	.393	.392	.391	.391
TS(*)	A tax adjustment parameter to reflect changes in tax law on the personal income tax receipts of the federal government.	.93	.93	.93	.93	.93	.93	.93	.93	.93	.93

*The asterisk should be replaced with the column number corresponding to the year in which the parameter's preset value is to be changed. For example, the 1972 value of ITC is 1. If the user desires to change this value to zero, he should enter ITC(2) = 0, as data.

or the user could enter:

Δ\$PARAMΔ S=0.09, FIBTR=0.035, DEPA(3)=0.0242, TS(2)=0.90, \$[CR]

or

Δ\$PARAM ΔFIBTR=0.035,[CR]
ΔS=0.09, TS(2)=0.90,[CR]
ΔDEPA(3)=0.0242,\$[CR]

The three different ways of entering the data indicate that (a) order is unimportant and that (b) data entries may continue on additional lines.[50] Following any *one* of the above three entries, the program requests data verification:

DATA OK?   (OK OR NO)

If the user responds with NO, the program will request the same data again; otherwise, the program continues with the next step. One valid response follows:

OK[CR]

Upon the successful completion of step 3, the program reaches the final major data section and indicates this with the following message:

4.   EXOG   LIST AND/OR CHANGE   (LO, CO, LC, OR NO)

The AEI model employs various exogenous variables in making a projection. Each of the exogenous variables are preset with "programmed" initial values which the user may modify in this section. As before, any initial values entered by the user will be maintained on all subsequent runs. The above message requests that the user direct the program to perform one of four operations on the preset values of the model's exogenous variables. As in step 3, the user should respond with one of the four operation codes enclosed in the parenthesis. Each code represents the same operation described in step 3 with the word "exogenous" substituted everywhere the word "parameter" appears. One valid response would be:

CO[CR]

The program would then reply with the data request message below:

DATA   (SPACE\$EXOG   VN1 =9.9, VN2=9.9, \$)

Following the above, the program is ready to accept user-supplied values for the exogenous variables, of which there are different types:

(a)   A number of equations in the model require 1971 values as starting points from which later values of the same variable are calculated.[51] Exogenous variables of this type appear in Table 12 as VNAME(1), which means variable name in period one, i.e., 1971.

(b)   Other exogenous variables, such as population, are in some sense "objective" and are, presumably, not affected by policy decisions.

(c)   Some variables, such as exports and imports, are essentially economic but are left exogenous since models external to the AEI model can easily generate the values to be inputted to the AEI model.

(d)   Finally, there are exogenous variables which are directly controlled by the federal government. These are of two forms, real and nominal. All federal or state-local purchases which are inputted must be in constant 1971 dollars. All exogenous transfers, grants, and contributions for social insurance should be given in current dollars consistent with the operating inflation assumption. All dollar amounts should be entered in billions of dollars (i.e., 900 million dollars would be inputted as 0.9).

As in step 3, each exogenous variable must be identified by means of a variable name the program recognizes. These variables are presented in Table 12 along with their economic names, a description of their functions and their "programmed" initial values.

Immediately following each variable name that is entered as data, there must appear an equals sign, the user's value for the variable, and a comma. Taking an illustrative example, suppose that the user desires to make the following changes:

Economic Name & Description	Variable Name	"Programmed" Initial Value	User's New Value
Housing starts in 1978	HS	2.40	2.45
Average cost of a housing unit in all years	HC	15.53	15.75
Net interest paid by consumers in 1971	PINT	17.60	17.50
Imports in 1975	MPT	0.0	107.50
1976		0.0	116.90
1977		0.0	126.70
1978		0.0	135.60
1979		0.0	145.20
1980		0.0	156.30

Table 12
VARIABLE NAME, ECONOMIC NAME, DESCRIPTION, AND PROGRAMMED INITIAL VALUES FOR THE EXOGENOUS VARIABLES IN THE AEI MODEL

Variable Name	Economic Name and Description	Programmed Initial Value									
		1 / 71	2 / 72	3 / 73	4 / 74	5 / 75	6 / 76	7 / 77	8 / 78	9 / 79	10 / 80
CHI	Contributions for HI (including SMI payments). This must be in current dollars consistent with the operative inflation assumption.[a]	0.0	0.0	0.0	0.0	0.0	0.0	0.0	0.0	0.0	0.0
COASDI	Contributions for social security except HI (Medicare). This must be in current dollars consistent with the operative inflation assumption.[a]	38.00	44.00	50.60	73.90	79.80	85.80	91.60	101.9	109.1	117.2
COLPOP	The number of students (in thousands) projected to attend college in the fall of each year. This variable is used for computing the work load increase for state purchases of higher education.	7796	8119	8449	8792	9147	9457	9710	9930	10125	10284
ESPOP	The number of students (in thousands) projected to attend elementary and secondary school for each year. This variable is used for computing the work load increase for state and local purchases for elementary and secondary education.	50807	50415	49994	49538	49009	48621	48323	48107	47972	47968

[a]In the model run shown, all contributions for HI and railroad retirement were included under COASDI.

Table 12 — Continued

Variable Name	Economic Name and Description	Programmed Initial Value									
		1 71	2 72	3 73	4 74	5 75	6 76	7 77	8 78	9 79	10 80
FCSIO	Federal contribution for social insurance except COASDI and CHI above. This must be in current dollars consistent with the operative inflation assumption.	9.9	10.9	11.9	12.8	13.5	14.6	15.5	16.7	17.9	18.9
FECIV	Federal civilian employment, thousands of employees.	2000	2000	2020	2017	2030	2000	2030	2050	2070	2100
FEAF	Armed forces employment, thousands of employees.	2490	2490	2396	2300	2200	2100	2100	2100	2100	2100
FINT(1)	Net interest paid by the federal government in current dollars.	14.3	14.7	15.1	15.5	15.5	15.2	14.9	14.6	14.3	13.9
FPRDF	Federal purchases for defense, billions of 1971 dollars.	75.0	75.0	74.0	73.0	69.4	70.4	71.4	71.0	69.5	69.2
FPRO	Federal nondefense purchases, billions of 1971 dollars.	23.0	21.4	25.0	26.0	37.1	36.0	36.3	37.2	38.1	38.9
FSUBLS	Federal subsidies less current surplus of government enterprises. These must be in current dollars consistent with the operative inflation assumption.	5.2	5.6	6.0	6.6	5.9	6.1	6.0	5.9	5.9	5.9

Variable Name	Economic Name and Description	Programmed Initial Value									
		1	2	3	4	5	6	7	8	9	10
		71	72	73	74	75	76	77	78	79	80
GPGNPD	Annual rate of growth of the private GNP deflator in decimal form (i.e., 2.7% = 0.027). 1971 must be 0.0	0.0	0.026	0.025	0.025	0.025	0.025	0.025	0.025	0.025	0.025
GRNTS	Grants to state and local governments. This must be in current dollars consistent with the operative inflation assumption.	29.0	32.0	36.0	40.0	44.5	46.7	49.6	52.0	54.6	57.4
HC	Average cost of a new housing unit in 1958 dollars. Employed as the average cost of a new housing unit throughout the projection.	15.53	15.53	15.53	15.53	15.53	15.53	15.53	15.53	15.53	15.53
HI[b]	Health insurance (Medicare) benefits, current dollars consistent with operative inflation assumption	0.0	0.0	0.0	0.0	0.0	0.0	0.0	0.0	0.0	0.0
HS	Housing starts, in millions.	2.1	2.0	2.1	2.2	2.3	2.3	2.4	2.4	2.5	2.5
IBT(1)	Total indirect business taxes, less state property taxes in 1971. Set other years to 0.0.	72.7	0.0	0.0	0.0	0.0	0.0	0.0	0.0	0.0	0.0
LFT	Total labor force, age 16 and over, in thousands.	86900	88100	90000	91800	93300	94900	96600	98200	99800	101400

[b]In the run shown, all federal transfer payments are given as OASDI (below).

Table 12 – Continued

Variable Name	Economic Name and Description	Programmed Initial Value									
		1 71	2 72	3 73	4 74	5 75	6 76	7 77	8 78	9 79	10 80
MPT	Imports, in constant 1971 dollars.	0.0	0.0	0.0	0.0	0.0	0.0	0.0	0.0	0.0	0.0
OASDI[c]	Social security benefits except HI (Medicare). This must be in current dollars consistent with the operative inflation assumption.	70.0	82.0	95.0	108.0	113.5	122.4	130.9	140.5	151.0	162.3
OTRF	Other federal transfer payments (except OASDHI), current dollars consistent with operative inflation assumption.	0.0	0.0	0.0	0.0	0.0	0.0	0.0	0.0	0.0	0.0
PINT(1)	Net interest paid by consumers. A 1971 value is needed in the calculations of the iterative block.	17.6	0.0	0.0	0.0	0.0	0.0	0.0	0.0	0.0	0.0
POP	Total population, in thousands.	206886	209016	211195	213424	215703	218301	220407	222828	225282	227765
PRODR	Annual rate of increase in private productivity in decimal form (i.e., 3.7% = 0.037). 1971 must be 0.0	0.0	0.050	0.042	0.035	0.030	0.030	0.030	0.030	0.030	0.030
SEAO	State and local employment, in thousands, *above* the baseline path.	0.0	0.0	0.0	0.0	0.0	0.0	0.0	0.0	0.0	0.0
SINT	Net interest paid by state and local governments, in current dollars.	0.4	0.4	0.4	0.4	0.4	0.4	0.4	0.4	0.4	0.4

[c]In the run shown, OASDI includes all federal transfers to persons as well as foreigners.

Variable Name	Economic Name and Description	Programmed Initial Value									
		1 71	2 72	3 73	4 74	5 75	6 76	7 77	8 78	9 79	10 80
SPCOLB(1)	State and local purchases for higher education in calendar year 1971, in current dollars. Other years should be set to 0.0.	12.00	0.0	0.0	0.0	0.0	0.0	0.0	0.0	0.0	0.0
SPESB(1)	State and local purchases for elementary and secondary education, calendar year 1971, in current dollars. Others years should be set to 0.0	42.60	0.0	0.0	0.0	0.0	0.0	0.0	0.0	0.0	0.0
SPNEB(1)	State and local purchases of everything else but the two catagories directly above. 1971 amount in current dollars. Other years should be set to 0.0	80.80	0.0	0.0	0.0	0.0	0.0	0.0	0.0	0.0	0.0
SPRAO	State and local purchases above the projected baseline. Amounts in constant 1971 dollars.	0.0	0.0	0.0	0.0	0.0	0.0	0.0	0.0	0.0	0.0
SSURPE(1)	State and local current surplus of government enterprises, in 1971, in current dollars. Other years should be set to 0.0	4.10	0.0	0.0	0.0	0.0	0.0	0.0	0.0	0.0	0.0

Table 12 – Continued

Variable Name	Economic Name and Description	Programmed Initial Value									
		1 71	2 72	3 73	4 74	5 75	6 76	7 77	8 78	9 79	10 80
STPNIA(1)	State and local personal taxes and nontaxes, NIA basis, current dollars, 1971 amount. Employed as an initial value in the revenue equations for state and local governments. Other years should be set to 0.0	27.40	0.0	0.0	0.0	0.0	0.0	0.0	0.0	0.0	0.0
STRFAO	An add-on to the baseline path of state transfers (excluding public assistance) which is calculated in the state and local sector of the model. Amounts must be given in current dollars consistent with the operative inflation assumption.	0.0	0.0	0.0	0.0	0.0	0.0	0.0	0.0	0.0	0.0
STRFPA	State and local transfers for public assistance, in current dollars, consistent with the operative inflation assumption. At present, all of public assistance appears as state and local transfers in the national income accounts.	9.3	10.2	11.2	12.3	9.0	9.8	10.5	11.1	11.8	12.4
UR	Unemployment rate, in decimal form.	0.060	0.056	0.046	0.040	0.040	0.040	0.040	0.040	0.040	0.040
XPT	Exports, in constant 1971 dollars.	0.0	0.0	0.0	0.0	0.0	0.0	0.0	0.0	0.0	0.0

To accomplish the above, the user would respond with:

$\triangle$$EXOG   HS(8)=2.45, HC(1)=10*15.75, PINT(1)=17.50,[CR]

$\triangle$ MPT(5)=107.5,116.9,126.7,135.6,145.2,156.3, $[CR]

Following the above entry, the program requests data verification:

DATA OK?   (OK OR NO)

The user should reply appropriately; for example:

OK[CR]

At this point, the program has reached the end of the data input section and conveys this to the user with the following message:

5.   END OF DATA   REPEAT STEP?   (OK OR NO)

Here the program is giving the user a "last chance" to go back to any one of the earlier steps and correct data that was inappropriately entered or to enter data that was inadvertently left out. If the user responds with NO[CR], the program will continue with step 6. A user response of OK[CR] will result in the message below:

DATA   ENTER   STEP NO (1,2,3 OR 4)

The user should respond to this data request with the number of the step he desires to repeat. For example, if the title in step 2 was incorrectly entered, the user would respond with:

2[CR]

Following this entry, the program will branch back and re-execute step 2 in its entirety. When step 2 is completed, the program will not continue with step 3, but will return to the beginning of step 5.

This point in the program is executed when the user response in step 5 is NO. Hence, all of the inputted data will have been entered correctly and the program will make the following request:

6.   LIST INPUT DATA   (OK OR NO)

If the user wants a listing of all the values assigned to the parameters and exogenous variables then he should reply with OK[CR] and the program will generate two 8-1/2 x 11 pages containing this information. Otherwise, the user should respond with NO[CR].

After a response of OK followed by the listing or a response of NO, the program will indicate that it has started the projection by printing:

RUNNING ———

No user responses are required until the projection is completed and all the tables in the output have been printed. Once this has occurred, the program will begin step 7.

Upon completion of the output generated by the projection, the program will make the following request:

7. TRACE OF OTHER ENDOG VARIABLES (OK OR NO)

During the projection, the model generates values for 125 endogenous variables of which a subset was printed in the output. The user may want to examine the values of some of the other endogenous variables that have not been printed out yet. In addition, the endogenous variables that are printed in the generated tables contain values for 1975 through 1980; therefore the user may want to examine the values of these variables prior to 1975. If the user does not elect to use this option, he should respond with NO[CR] and the program will continue at step 8; otherwise, he should enter OK[CR] and the program will make its next request:

DATA   ENTER   BEGIN YEAR/END YEAR (99/99)

Since the user may not want to examine all the values of an endogenous variable between 1971 and 1980, it would be inefficient to print more than the period he wishes to examine. Thus, the above message requests that the user enter the last two digits of the year marking the beginning of the period he wants to examine, followed by a slash (/), and the last two digits of the year marking the ending of the period. For example, suppose that the user desires to examine some of the other endogenous variables between 1975 and 1980. In this case, he would respond with:

75/80[CR]

Immediately thereafter, the program would respond with the messages below:

DATA   ENTER VARIABLE NAME (XXXXXXXX)
YOU MUST ENTER 8 CHARACTERS

Following this message, the user may enter any one of the following:

a variable name[CR]   Any of the 125 variable names in Table 13.

ALL [CR]   This response will cause all the variables from the current point in Table 13 through the end of Table 13 to be listed.

FINISH [CR]   This response directs the program to go to step 8.

To illustrate this feature, suppose that the user wants to examine all of the deflators. Initially, the program has a pointer positioned at the top of Table 13, that is, at the variable name FINT. This pointer must be moved from FINT to the variable name for the first deflator, FPRD, in order to obtain its values. This operation is performed when the user enters:

$$FPRD\triangle\triangle\triangle\triangle\,[CR]$$

Immediately following the user's response, the program will print the values of the federal purchases deflator between 1975 and 1980. The program then positions the pointer at the next variable name, FPRD58. To obtain the remaining deflators, the user could then enter FPRD58 as his second response, GNPD as his third response, and so on through XPTD58.

This procedure, however, is time-consuming and the user can avoid it by entering:

$$ALL\triangle\triangle\triangle\triangle\triangle\,[CR]$$

Following this response, the program will list the 1975 to 1980 values of all the deflators beginning with FPRD58 and ending with XPTD58. After the values of XPTD58 have been listed, the program will position the pointer at the top of Table 13 and the user may select other variables to be listed or respond with FINISH, in which case the program will continue at step 8.

One final note is in order. If after entering a variable name, the program responds with:

Variable Name NOT FOUND, TRY AGAIN

then the user has either misspelled the variable name or requested a variable name that does not exist in Table 13.

At this point, the program has completed one run of the AEI model and makes its final request for this run:

8. LAST RUN   (OK OR NO)

If the user desires to make an additional run, he should enter NO [CR] and the program will begin again at step 2. Otherwise, he should enter OK [CR] and execution of the program will terminate.

Leaving the Computer System. When the AEI model terminates execution, the computer system will inform the user to this effect by responding with the following:

CPU TIME: 15.81   ELAPSED TIME: 47:48.17

EXIT

The user can now leave the computer system by responding with:

.KJOB[CR]

The computer system will respond with:

CONFIRM:

The above message requests confirmation of the status to be given the files (created by the user) after the logout is complete. The user has the option of responding with several different codes. (See Table 13.)

Table 13
ENDOGENOUS VARIABLES

Variable Name	Description	
FINT	Federal interest payments	
FSURP	Federal surplus	
IBT	Indirect business taxes, total	
PINT	Personal interest payments	
SPCOLB	State purchases, college, baseline	LAGGED 71
SPESB	State purchases, elementary & secondary, baseline	
SPNEB	State purchases, noneducational, baseline	
SSURPE	State current surplus of government enterprise	
STPNIA	State personal taxes, NIA	
BFI	Business fixed investment, real	
BFIN	Business fixed investment, nominal	
FD	Final demand, real	
FDN	Final demand, nominal	
FPR	Federal purchases, real	
FPRDFN	Federal purchases, defense, nominal	PRODUCT SIDE
FPRN	Federal purchases, nominal	
FPRON	Federal purchases, other, nominal	
GAP	Demand gap, real	
GAPN	Demand gap, nominal	
GNP	Gross national product, real	

Table 13 — Continued

Variable Name	Description
GNPN	Gross national product, nominal
INVI	Inventory investment, real
INVIN	Inventory investment, nominal
MPTN	Imports, nominal
NETXM	Net exports-imports, real
NETXMN	Net exports-imports, nominal
NPT	Necessary personal tax increase, real
NPTN	Necessary personal tax increase, nominal
PCE	Personal consumption expenditures, real
PCEN	Personal consumption expenditures, nominal
PDE	Producers' durable equipment, real
PDEN	Producers' durable equipment, nominal
PS	Producers' structures, real
PSN	Producers' structures, nominal
RCI	Residential construction investment, real
RCIN	Residential construction investment, nominal
SPR	State purchases, real
SPRB	State purchases, baseline
SPRN	State purchases, nominal
VATR	Value added tax rate, real
VATRN	Value added tax rate, nominal
XPTN	Exports, nominal
CCF	Corporate cash flow
CCCA	Corporate capital consumption allowances
CHI	Contributions to HI
CIVA	Corporate inventory valuation adjustment
COASDI	Contributions to OASDI
CP	Corporate profits
CPCIVA	Corporate profits & corporate IVA
CSI	Contributions to social insurance, total
DEFERR	Deflator error
DIV	Dividends
DPY	Disposable personal income
ECIV	Employment, civilian
FCSI	Federal contributions to social insurance
FCT	Federal corporate taxes
FFA	Federal foreign aid
FGNP58	Federal GNP, $58
FIBT	Federal indirect business taxes
FTPNIA	Federal personal taxes, NIA
FTRF	Federal transfer payments

PRODUCT SIDE

INCOME SIDE & OTHERS

Table 13 — Continued

Variable Name	Description
GI	Gross investment
GNP58	GNP, $58
GPCEPC	Growth rate of personal consumption expenditure, per capita
GPCEPG	Growth rate of personal consumption expenditure, per capita (with GAP filled)
GSURP	Government surplus or deficit
INT	Interest payments, total
LFCIV	Labor force, civilian
NCCCA	Noncorporate capital consumption allowances
NNP	Net national product
PCEG	Personal consumption expenditures, GAP filled
PCEPC	Personal consumption expenditures, per capita
PCEPCG	Personal consumption expenditures, per capita, GAP filled
PCER	Personal consumption expenditures as a share of GNP
PCERG	Personal consumption expenditures as a share of GNP, GAP filled
PCSI	Personal contributions to social insurance
PE	Private employment
PERSAV	Personal savings
PGNP58	Private GNP, $58
PGROW	Rate of growth of prices
PNGR	Ratio of private GNP to GNP
POPWRK	GNP per private worker, $58
PRODIN	Productivity index
RGROW	Rate of growth of real GNP
SCSI	State contributions to social insurance
SCT	State corporate taxes
SEB	State employment, baseline
SGNP58	State GNP, $58
SIBT	State indirect business taxes
SPT	State property tax
SSURP	State budget surplus
STRF	State transfers, total
STRFO	State transfers, other
SUBLS	Subsidies less current surplus of government enterprise, total
SURP	Federal budget surplus if taxes are changed to eliminate GAP
TOTL3E	Total expenditures, Table 3
TOTL3R	Total receipts, Table 3
TOTL5E	Total expenditures, Table 5
TOTL5R	Total receipts, Table 5
TOTL6S	Total savings, Table 6
TPNIA	Total federal & state personal taxes, NIA
TPSOI	Personal taxes under current law, SOI
TRF	Transfers, total

INCOME SIDE & OTHERS

Table 13 — Continued

Variable Name	Description	
TRF3	Transfers, total & FFA	
UNDCP	Undistributed corporate profits	
YPT	Taxable personal income	
FPRD	Federal purchases deflator	
FPRD58	Federal purchases deflator, $58	
GNPD	GNP deflator	
GNPD58	GNP deflator, $58	
MPTD	Imports deflator	
MPTD58	Imports deflator, $58	
PCED	Personal consumption expenditures deflator	
PCED58	Personal consumption expenditures deflator, $58	DEFLATORS
PDED	Producers' durables & equipment deflator	
PDED58	Producers' durables & equipment deflator, $58	
PGNPD	Private GNP deflator	
PSD	Producers' structures deflator	
PSD58	Producers' structures deflator, $58	
RCID	Residential construction investment deflator	
RCID58	Residential construction investment deflator, $58	
SPRD	State purchases deflator	
SPRD58	State purchases deflator, $58	
XPTD	Exports deflator	
XPTD58	Exports deflator, $58	

However, the following response:

CONFIRM: P[CR]

will preserve all but .TMP files.

The computer system will respond with accounting information and other wrap-up messages before logical disconnection. When the disconnect is complete, the indicator lamp, referred to above, will go out. All that remains is to remove the phone from the acoustic coupler, hang up, and turn the terminal's power switch to "off."

Sample Run of the Model

The run of the model used in the "Options Volume" is presented below to illustrate the product of the steps described in the previous section, and to allow for a brief discussion of how some of the output tables should be interpreted in describing budget policies.

```
PLEASE LOGIN OR ATTACH
.LOGIN 2327,506
JOB 5  W A C C C  505(32)  TTY14
PASSWORD:
1258       24-MAR-73     SAT

.RUN MODEL

LRBP MODEL  VERSION 03/24/73
FAMILIAR WITH PROG? (OK OR NO)

NO

1. DATE ENTER AS (99/99/99)

03/24/73

DATA OK? (OK OR NO)

OK

2. TITLE ENTER UP TO 48 CHARACTERS

ADMN. UPDATE : 4.0% UNEMPLOY; 0.07 SAVINGS

DATA OK? (OK OR NO)

OK

3. PARAM LIST AND/OR CHANGE (LO,CO,LC, OR NO)

NO

4.EXOG  LIST AND/OR CHANGE (LO,CO,LC, OR NO)

NO

5. END  OF DATA REPEAT STEP? (OK OR NO)

NO

6. LIST INPUT DATA (OK OR NO)

OK
```

INITIAL VALUES PARAM LIST

--CCCAR---	---CFR----	--CIVA71--	---COLER--	---EDIT---	---EPS----
0.35600	0.16000	-4.70000	0.81000	0.00000	0.00100

---FIBTR/-	---ITERL--	---PIP----	-----S----	---SIBTR--
0.02800	10.00000	0.02500	0.07000	0.06200

---SPTR---	---TNIA---
0.03800	0.05000

YR	----CTP---	---DEPA---	---ITC----	---SPRB---	---TRC----	----TS----
71	0.000	0.010	1.000	135.400	0.424	0.930
72	0.000	0.018	1.000	0.000	0.410	0.930
73	0.000	0.024	1.000	0.000	0.400	0.930
74	0.000	0.026	1.000	0.000	0.415	0.930
75	-0.400	0.029	1.000	0.000	0.394	0.930
76	-0.400	0.029	1.000	0.000	0.394	0.930
77	-0.400	0.025	1.000	0.000	0.393	0.930
78	-0.400	0.022	1.000	0.000	0.392	0.930
79	-0.400	0.020	1.000	0.000	0.391	0.930
80	-0.400	0.018	1.000	0.000	0.391	0.930

INITIAL VALUES EXOG LIST

YR	---CHI----	--COASDI--	--COLPOP--	--ESPOP---	--FCSIO---	---FECIV--
71	0.000	38.000	7796.000	50807.000	9.900	2000.000
72	0.000	44.000	8119.000	50415.000	10.900	2000.000
73	0.000	50.600	8449.000	49994.000	11.900	2020.000
74	0.000	73.900	8792.000	49538.000	12.800	2017.000
75	0.000	79.800	9147.000	49009.000	13.500	2030.000
76	0.000	85.800	9457.000	48621.000	14.600	2000.000
77	0.000	91.600	9710.000	48323.000	15.500	2030.000
78	0.000	101.900	9930.000	48107.000	16.700	2050.000
79	0.000	109.100	10125.000	47972.000	17.900	2070.000
80	0.000	117.200	10284.000	47968.000	18.900	2100.000

YR	-/-FEAF---	---FINT---	--FPRDF---	---FPRO---	--FSULS--	--GPGNPD/-
71	2490.000	14.300	75.000	23.000	5.200	0.000
72	2490.000	14.700	75.000	21.400	5.600	0.026
73	2396.000	15.100	74.000	25.000	6.000	0.025
74	2300.000	15.500	73.000	26.000	6.600	0.025
75	2200.000	15.500	69.400	37.100	5.900	0.025
76	2100.000	15.200	70.400	36.000	6.100	0.025
77	2100.000	14.900	71.400	36.300	6.000	0.025
78	2100.000	14.600	71.000	37.200	5.900	0.025
79	2100.000	14.300	69.500	38.100	5.900	0.025
80	2100.000	13.900	69.200	38.900	5.900	0.025

YR	--GRNTS---	----HC----	----HI----	----HS----	---IBT----	---LFT----
71	29.000	15.530	0.000	2.100	72.700	86900.000
72	32.000	15.530	0.000	2.000	0.000	88100.000
73	36.000	15.530	0.000	2.100	0.000	90000.000
74	40.000	15.530	0.000	2.200	0.000	91800.000
75	44.500	15.530	0.000	2.300	0.000	93300.000
76	46.700	15.530	0.000	2.300	0.000	94900.000
77	49.600	15.530	0.000	2.400	0.000	96600.000
78	52.000	15.530	0.000	2.400	0.000	98200.000
79	54.600	15.530	0.000	2.500	0.000	99800.000
80	57.400	15.530	0.000	2.500	0.000	101400.000

YR	---MPT----	--OASDI---	---OTRF---	---PINT---	---POP----	--PRODR---
71	0.000	70.000	0.000	17.600	206886.000	0.000
72	0.000	82.000	P.000	0.000	209016.000	0.042
73	0.000	95.000	0.000	0.000	211195.000	0.040
74	0.000	108.000	0.000	0.000	213424.000	0.035
75	0.000	113.500	0.000	0.000	215703.000	0.030
76	0.000	122.400	0.000	0.000	218301.000	0.030
77	0.000	130.;00	0.000	0.000	220407.000	0.030
78	0.000	140.500	0.000	0.000	222828.000	0.030
79	0.000	151.000	0.000	0.000	225282.000	0.030
80	0.000	162.300	0.000	0.000	227765.000	0.030

YR	---SEAO---	---SINT---	=-SPCOLB--	--SPESB---	--SPNEB---	=-SPRAO-/-
71	0.000	0.400	12.000	42.600	80.800	0.000
72	0.000	0.400	0.000	0.000	0.000	0.000
73	0.000	0.400	0.000	0.000	0.000	0.000
74	0.000	0.400	0.000	0.000	0.000	0.000
75	0.000	0.400	0.000	0.000	0.000	0.000
76	0.000	0.400	0.000	0.000	0.000	0.000
77	0.000	0.400	0.000	0.000	0.000	0.000
78	0.000	0.400	0.000	0.000	0.000	0.000
79	0.000	0.400	0.000	0.000	0.000	0.000
80	0.000	0.400	0.000	0.000	0.000	0.000

YR	--SSURPE--	--STPNIA--	--STRFAO--	--STRFPA--	----UR----	---XPT----
71	4.100	27.400	0.000	9.300	0.060	0.000
72	0.000	0.000	0.000	10.200	0.056	0.000
73	0.000	0.000	0.000	11.200	0.046	0.000
74	0.000	0.000	0.000	12.300	0.040	0.000
75	0.000	0.000	0.000	9.000	0.040	0.000
76	0.000	0.000	0.000	9.800	0.040	0.000
77	0.000	0.000	0.000	10.500	0.040	0.000
78	0.000	0.000	0.000	11.100	0.040	0.000
79	0.000	0.000	0.000	11.800	0.040	0.000
80	0.000	0.000	0.000	12.400	0.040	0.000

RUNNING---

*** PRODUCT SIDE IN 1971 DOLLARS **

	1975	1976	1977	1978	1979	198*
GROSS NATIONAL PRODUCT	1287.0	1345.3	1406.0	1467.2	1530.5	1595.8
CONSUMPTION	792.3	825.8	860.3	892.5	928.6	965.6
BUSINESS FIXED INVEST	148.3	155.3	162.6	169.9	177.4	185.1
INVENTORY INVESTMENT	14.3	15.0	15.7	16.4	17.2	17.9
RESIDENTAL CONSTRUCTION	53.8	53.8	56.1	56.1	58.5	58.5
NET EXPORTS	0.0	0.0	0.0	0.0	0.0	0.0
FEDERAL PURCHASES	106.5	106.4	107.7	108.2	107.6	108.1
DEFENSE	69.4	70.4	71.4	71.0	69.5	69.2
OTHER	37.1	36.0	36.3	37.2	38.1	38.9
STATE & LOCAL PURCHASES	156.3	162.2	168.1	174.4	181.0	188.0
FINAL DEMAND	1271.5	1318.6	1370.5	1417.5	1470.2	1523.2
GAP	-15.5	-26.7	-35.5	-49.7	-60.3	-72.6
NECESSARY TAX INCREASE	-18.8	-32.5	-43.3	-60.9	-74.1	-89.5
VALUE ADDED RATE	-.0238	-.0394	-.0504	-.0682	-.0798	-.0927

*** PRODUCT SIDE IN CURRENT DOLLARS ***

	1975	1976	1977	1978	1979	198*
GROSS NATIONAL PRODUCT	1435.8	1541.3	1655.2	1774.9	1902.6	2038.8
CONSUMPTION	871.9	930.1	992.2	1054.1	1123.3	1196.6
BUSINESS FIXED INVEST	163.5	175.6	188.5	202.0	216.4	231.7
INVENTORY INVESTMENT	15.9	17.0	18.3	19.6	20.9	22.4
RESIDENTAL CONSTRUCTION	60.9	62.7	67.3	69.3	74.3	765
NET EXPORTS	0.0	0.0	0.0	0.0	0.0	0.0
FEDERAL PURCHASES	120.7	124.5	130.1	135.0	138.6	143.7
DEFENSE	78.7	82.4	86.3	88.6	89.5	92.0
OTHER	42.1	42.1	43.9	46.4	49.1	51.7
STATE & LOCAL PURCHASES	185.6	200.8	217.0	234.8	254.1	275.2
FINAL DEMAND	1418.5	1510.7	1613.4	1714.8	1827.7	1946.1
GAP	-17.3	-30.6	-41.8	-60.1	-74.9	-92.7
NECESSARY TAX INCREASE	-20.7	-36.6	-50.0	-71.9	-89.6	-310.9
VALUE ADDED RATE	-.0238	=.0394	-.0504	-.0682	-.0798	-.0927

** FEDERAL BUDGET IN CURRENT DOLLARS **

	1975	1976	1977	1978	1979	198*
RECIEPTS						
PEVSONAL INCOME TAX	128.3	139.7	152.2	165.0	179.1	194.2
CONTRIBUTIONS SOCIAL INS	93.5	100.5	107.2	118.7	127.1	136.1
CORPORATE INCOME TAX	53.5	57.4	61.9	66.6	71.4	76.7
INDIRECT BUSINESS TAX	24.4	26.0	27.8	29.5	31.5	33.5
TOTAL RECIEPTS	299.7	323.7	349.1	379.8	409.0	440.6
EXPENDITURES						
TOTAL PURCHASES	120.7	124.5	130.1	135.0	138.6	143.7
DEFENSE	78.7	82.4	86.3	88.6	89.5	92.0
OTHER	42.1	42.1	43.9	46.4	49.1	51.7
TOTAL \RANSFERS	113.7	122.6	131.1	140.6	151.1	162.3
TO PERSONS	110.4	119.0	127.2	136.6	146.8	157.7
TO FOREIGNERS	3.3	3.5	3.8	4.0	4.3	4.6
GRANTS TO S&L GOVT´S	44.5	46.7	49.6	52.0	54.6	57.4
SUBSIDIES LESS SURPLUS	5.9	6.1	6.0	5.9	5.9	5.9
NET INTEREST P@ID	15.5	15.2	14.9	14.6	14.3	13.9
TOTAL EXPENDITURES	300.3	315.1	331.7	348.1	364.5	383.3
SURPLUS OP DEFICIT	-0.7	8.7	17.4	31.7	44.6	57.3
SURPLUS TO BALANCE ECO.	-21.4	-28.0	-32.6	-40.2	-45.1	=53.6

65

*** INCOME SIDE IN CURRGNT DOLLARS **

	1975	1976	1977	1978	1979	198*
GROSS NATIONAL PRODUCT	1435.8	1541.3	1655.2	1774.9	1902.6	2038.8
-NON CORP CAPCON ALLOWS	35.5	41.0	46.0	50.6	55.1	59.5
-CORP CAPCONS ALLOWANCE	88.7	95.2	101.1	107.4	114.5	122.0
=NET NATIONAL PRODUCT	1311.6	1405.1	1508.1	1616.8	1733.1	1857.4
-CONTRIBUTION SOCIAL INS	105.8	113.8	121.5	134.1	143.6	153.9
FEDERAL	93.5	100.5	107.2	118.7	127.1	136.1
STATE & LOCAL	12.3	13.3	14.3	15.4	16.5	17.8
-CORP PROFITS & IVA	141.5	151.8	164.0	176.8	190.1	204.3
+SUBSIDIES LESS SURPLUS	0.3	0.1	-0.5	-1.0	-1.5	-2.1
-INDIRECT BUSINESS TAXES	133.1	142.4	152.3	162.4	173.4	185.2
FEDERAL	24.4	26.0	27.8	29.5	31.5	33.5
STATE & LOCAL	108.7	116.3	124.5	132.9	142.0	151.7
+DIVIDENDS	37.0	41.7	46.0	50.1	54.2	58.3
+NET INTEREST PAID	40.0	41.3	42.8	44.2	45.8	47.4
PERSONAL	24.1	25.7	27.4	29.2	31.1	33.1
FEDERAL	15.5	15.2	14.9	14.6	14.3	13.9
STATE & LOCAL	0.4	0.4	0.4	0.4	0.4	0.4
+TRANSFERS	127.9	138.0	147.6	158.3	170.0	182.4
FEDERAL	110.4	119.0	127.2	136.6	146.8	157.7
STATE & LOCAL	17.5	19.0	20.4	21.7	23.2	24.7
-PARSONAL TAX & NONTAX	174.5	191.6	210.6	230.6	252.7	2767
FEDERAL	128.3	139.7	152.2	165.0	179.1	194.2
STATE & LOCAL	46.2	51.9	58.4	65.6	73.6	82.5
=DISPOSABLE PERSONAL INC	964.5	1028.9	1097.6	1166.1	1242.6	1323.6

STATE & LOCAL BUDGET IN CURRENT DOLLARS

	1975	1976	1977	1978	1979	198*
RECIEPTS						
PERSONAL TAX & NONTAX	46.2	51.9	78.4	65.6	73.6	82.5
+INDIRECT BUSINESS TXES	108.7	116.3	124.5	132.9	142.0	151.7
+CORPORATE TAXES	6.0	6.5	7.3	7.6	8.3	8.9
+CONTRIBUTION SOCIAL INS	12.3	13.3	14.3	15>4	16.5	17.8
+GRANTS	44.5	46.7	49.6	52.0	54.6	57.4
=TOTAL RECIEPTS	217.7	234.7	653.9	273.4	294.9	318.3
EXPENDITURES						
PURCHASES	185.6	200.8	217.0	234.8	254.1	275.2
+TRANSFERS	17.5	19.0	20.4	21.7	23.2	24.7
+NET INTEREST PAID	0.4	0.4	0.4	0.4	0.4	0.4
-SURPLUS OF GOVT ENTPR	5.6	6.0	6.5	6.9	7.4	8.0
=TOTAL EXPENDITURES	197.9	214.1	231.3	249.9	270.3	292.3
SURPLUS OR DEFICIT(-)	19.8	20.6	22.6	23.5	24.7	26.0

*** SAVINGS   INVESTMENT BALANCE ***

	1975	1976	1977	1978	1979	198*
GROSS PRIVATE SAVING						
PERSONAL SAVING	67.5	72.0	76.8	81.6	87.0	92.7
UNDIST CORP PROFITS	51.2	52.8	56.1	60.1	64.4	69.0
CORPORATE IVA	-6.2	-6.7	-7.2	-7.6	-8.1	-8.7
CORP CAPCONS ALLOWANCE	88.7	95.2	101.3	107.4	114.5	122.0
NON CORP CAPCON ALLOWS	35.5	41.0	46.0	50.6	55.1	59.5
TOTAL SAVING	236.7	274.3	272.9	292.1	312.8	334.4
GOV'T SURPLUS OR DEFICIT	19.1	29.2	40.0	55.2	69.2	83.3
GROSS INVESTMENT	240.3	255.3	274.3	290.9	311.6	330.6

*** PERSONAL CONSUMPTION STATISTICS ***J

	1975	1976	1977	1978	1979	198*
WITH GAP UNFILLED						
PERSONAL CONSUMPTION 71$	792.3	825.8	860.3	892.5	928.6	965.6
PERCAPITA CONSUMPTIN 71$	3673.3	3783.1	3903.1	4005.1	4121.8	4239.4
GROWTH RATE	1.0232	1.0299	1.0317	1.0261	1.0291	1.0285
CONSUMPTION /GNP	.6156	.6139	.6119	.6083	.6067	.6051
WITH GAP FILLED BY CONSWMPTION						
PERSONAL CONSUMPTION 71$	807.9	852.6	895.8	942.2	988.8	1038.2
PERCAPITA CONSUMPTIN 71$	3745.3	3905.5	4064.2	4228.2	4389.4	4558.1
GROWTH RATE	1.0300	1.0428	1.0406	1.0404	1.0381	1.0384
CONSUMPTION /GNP	.6277	.6337	.6371	.6422	.6461	.6506

7. TRACE OF OTHER ENDOG VARIABLES (OK OR NO)

OK

DATA   ENTER BEGIN YEAR/END YEAR (99/99)

75/80

DATA   ENTER VARIABLE NAME (XXXXXXXX)
YOU MUST ENTER 8 CHARACTERS

ALL

FINT
      15.5   15.2   14.9   14.6   14.3   13.9

FSURP
      -0.7   8.7   17.4   31.7   44.6   57.3

IBT
     133.1   142.4   152.3   162.4   173.4   185.2

PINT
      24.1   25.7   27.4   29.2   31.1   33.1

SPCOLB
      14.4   15.0   15.6   16.1   16.5   16.9

SPESB
      45.2   45.9   46.7   47.6   48.6   49.8

SPNEB
      96.7   101.3   105.8   110.7   115.9   121.2

SSURPE
       5.6   6.0   6.5   6.9   7.4   8.0

STPNIA
      46.2   51.9   58.4   65.6   73.6   82.5

BFI
     148.3   155.3   162.6   169.9   177.4   185.1

BFIN
     163.5   175.6   188.5   202.0   216.4   231.7

FD
    1271.5   1318.6   1370.5   1417.5   1470.2   1523.2

FDN
    1418.5   1510.7   1613.4   1714.8   1827.7   1946.1

FPR
     106.5   106.4   107.7   108.2   107.6   108.1

FPRDFN
      78.7   82.4   86.3   88.6   89.5   92.0

FPRN
     120.7   124.5   130.1   135.0   138.6   143.7

FPRON
      42.1   42.1   43.9   46.4   49.1   51.7

GAP
     -15.5   -26.7   -35.5   -49.7   -60.3   -72.6

GAPN
     -17.3   -30.6   -41.8   -60.1   -74.9   -92.7

GNP
    1287.0   1345.3   1406.0   1467.2   1530.5   1595.8

70

```
GNPN
   1435.8 1541.3 1655.2 1774.9 1902.6 2038.8

INVI
     14.3    15.0    15.7    16.4    17.2    17.9

INVIN
     15.9    17.0    18.3    19.6    20.9    22.4

MPTN
      0.0     0.0     0.0     0.0     0.0     0.0

NETXM
      0.0     0.0     0.0     0.0     0.0     0.0

NETXMN
      0.0     0.0     0.0     0.0     0.0     0.0

NPT
    -18.8   -32.5   -43.3   -60.9   /74.1   -89.5

NPTN
    -20.7   -36.6   -50.0   -71.9   -89.6  -110.9

PCE
    792.3   825.8   860.3   892.5   928.6   965.6

PCEN
    871.9   930.1   992.2  1054.1  1123.3  1196.6

PDE
    103.5   108.5   113.5   118.6   123.9   129.3

PDEN
    114.4   122.3   130.8   139.7   14;.1   159.0

PS
     44.7    46.9    49.0    51.2    53.5    55.8

PSN
     49.2    53.3    57.7    62.3    67.3    72.6

PCI
     53.8    53.8    56.1    56.1    58.5    58.5

PCIN
     60.9    62.7    67.3    69.3    74.3    76.5

SPR
    156.3   162.2   168.1   174.4   181.0   188.0

SPRB
    156.3   162.2   168.1   174.4   181.0   188.0

SPRN
    385.6   200.8   217.0   234.8   254.1   275.2

VATR
     -0.0    -0.0    -0.1    -0.1    -0.1    -0.1

VATRN
     -0.0    -0.0    -0.1    -0.1    -0.1    -0.1
```

XPTN
    0.0   0.0   0.0   0.0   0.0   0.0

CCF
  230.1 247.0 265.1 284.2 304.6 326.3

CCCA
   88.7   95.2 101.1 107.4 114.5 122.0

CHI
    0.0   0.0   0.0   0.0   0.0   0.0

CIVA
   -6.2   -6.7   -7.2   -7.6   -8.1   -8.7

COASDI
   79.9   85.9   91.7 102.0 109.2 117.2

CP
  147.6 158.5 171.2 184.4 198.2 212.9

CPCIVA
  141.5 151.8 164.0 176.8 190.1 204.3

CSI
  105.8 113.8 121.5 134.1 143.6 153.9

DEFERR
 1.0017 1.0014 1.0012 1.0008 1.0005 1.0001

DIV
   37.0   41.7   46.0   50.1   54.2   58.3

DPY
  964.5 1028.9 1097.6 1166.1 1242.6 1323.6

ECIV
 87456. 89088. 90720. 92256. 93792. 95328.

FCSI
   93.5 100.5 107.2 118.7 127.1 136.1

FCT
   53.5   57.4   61.9   66.6   71.4   76.7

FFA
    3.3   3.5   3.8   4.0   4.3   4.6

FGNP58
   20.1   19.5   19.6   19.7   19.8   19.9

FIBT
   24.4   26.0   27.8   29.5   31.5   33.5

FTPNIA
  128.3 139.7 152.2 165.0 179.1 194.2

FTRF
  110.4 119.0 127.2 136.6 146.8 157.7

GI
  240.3 255.3 274.1 290.9 311.6 330.6

GNP58
   908.9   950.1   992.9 1036.1 1080.8 1127.0

GPCEPC
     1.0   1.0   1.0   1.0   1.0   1.0

GPCEPG
     1.0   1.0   1.0   1.0   1.0   1.0

GSURP
    19.1   29.2   40.0   75.2   69.2   83.3

INT
    40.0   41.3   42.8   44.2   45.8   47.4

LFCIV
 91100. 92800. 94500. 96100. 97700. 99300.

NCCCA
    35.5   41.0   46.0   50.6   55.1   59.5

NNP
 1311.6 1405.1 1508.1 1616.8 1733.1 1857.4

PCEG
   807.9   852.6   895.8   942.2   988.8 1038.2

PCGPC
 3673.3 3783.1 3903.1 4005.1 4121.8 4239.4

PCEPCG
 3745.3 3905.5 4064.2 4228.2 4389.4 4578.1

PCER
     0.6   0.6   0.6   0.6   0.6   0.6

PCERG
     0.6   0.6   0.6   0.6   0.6   0.7

PCSI
    51.4   55.3   59.0   65.1   69.8   74.8

PE
 74088. 75357. 76568. 77670. 78753. 79803.

PERSAV
    67.5   72.0   76.8   81.6   87.0   92.7

PGNP58
   844.4   884.7   925.9   967.4 1010.3 1054.4

PGROW
   .0272   .0270   .0275   .0276   .0276   .0277

PNGR
   .9291   .9312   .9325   .9336   .9347   .9357

POPWRK
 1139.8 1174.0 1209.2 1245.5 1282.8 1321.3

PRODIN
 1.1553 1.1899 1.2256 1.2624 3.3003 1.3393

```
RGROW
    .0441    .0453    .0451    .0435    .0431    .0427

SCSI
    12.3     13.3     14.3     15.4     16.5     17.8

SCT
     6.0      6.5      7.1      7.6      8.3      8.9

SEB
 11338.   11731.   12122.   12536.   12969.   13425.

SGNP58
    44.4     45.9     47.5     49.1     50.8     52.6

SIBT
   108.7    116.3    124.5    132.9    142.0    151.7

SPT
    54.7     58.7     63.0     67.5     72.3     77.5

SSWRP
    19.8     20.6     22.6     23.5     24.7     26.0

STRF
    17.5     19.0     20.4     21.7     23.2     24.7

STRFO
     8.5      9.2      9.8     10.6     11.4     12.3

SUBLS
     0.3      0.1     -0.5     -1.0     -1.5     -2.1

SURP
   -21.4    -28.0    -32.6    -40.2    -45.1    -53.6

TOTL3E
   300.3    315.1    331.7    348.1    364.5    383.3

TOTL3R
   299.7    323.7    349.1    379.8    409.0    440.6

TOTL5E
   197.9    214.1    231.3    249.9    270.3    292.3

TOTL5R
   217.7    234.7    253.9    273.4    294.9    318.3

TOTL6S
   236.7    254.3    272.9    292.1    312.8    334.4

TPNIA
   174.5    191.6    210.6    230.6    252.7    276.7

TPSOI
   122.2    133.1    145.0    157.2    170.6    185.0

TRF
   127.9    138.0    147.6    158.3    170.0    182.4

TRF3
   113.7    122.6    131.1    140.6    151.1    162.3
```

UNDCP
   51.2   52.8   56.1   60.1   64.4   69.0

YPT
 1062.5 1137.8 1219.6 1303.6 1395.2 1492.7

FPRD
   1.13   1.17   1.21   1.25   1.29   1.33

FPRD58
   1.77   1.83   1.89   1.95   2.02   2.08

GNPD
   1.12   1.15   1.18   1.21   1.24   1.28

GNPD58
   1.58   1.62   1.67   1.71   1.76   1.81

MPTD
   5.91   6.05   6.21   6.37   6.53   6.70

MPTD58
   7.35   7.54   7.77   7.93   8.13   8.34

PCED
   1.10   1.12   1.15   1.18   1.21   1.24

PCED58
   1.48   1.51   1.55   1.59   1.63   1.67

PDED
   1.10   1.13   1.15   1.18   1.20   1.23

PDED58
   1.37   1.40   1.43   1.46   1.49   1.53

PGNPD
   1.10   1.13   1.16   1.19   1.22   1.25

PSD
   1.10   1.14   1.17   1.22   1.26   1.30

PSD58
   1.87   1.93   2.00   2.07   2.14   2.22

RCID
   1.13   1.16   1.20   1.23   1.27   1.31

RCID58
   1.70   1.75   1.80   1.85   1.91   1.97

SPRD
   1.19   1.24   1.29   1.34   1.40   1.46

SPRD58
   2.04   2.11   2.19   2.28   2.36   2.45

XPTD
   1.05   1.07   1.09   1.11   1.13   1.16

XPTD58
   1.32   1.35   1.37   1.40   1.43   1.46

```
DATA    ENTER VARIABLE NAME (XXXXXXXX)
YOU MUST ENTER 8 CHARACTERS

FINISH

8. LAST RUN (OK OR NO)

OK

CPU TIME: 14.25 ELAPSED TIME: 47:24.22

EXIT

.KJOB
CONFIRM: P
JOB 5, USER [2327,506] LOGGED OFF TTY14      1346  24-MAR-73
SAVED ALL FILES (240 BLOCKS)
RUNTIME 0 MIN, 14.98 SEC
```

A Note on Interpretation of the GAP Shown in the Output

The GAP shown in the output is defined as the difference between final demand and potential supply. If the GAP is positive, it means that the demand for use of the nation's output exceeds the potential supply of output. If the GAP is negative, it means that there is excess supply. The necessary tax increase, which is presented in the product-side tables just after the GAP itself, represents the dollar amount that federal personal taxes would have to be increased in order to change personal consumption expenditures by an amount just equal to, and opposite in sign from, the GAP, thereby eliminating the GAP. The federal surplus necessary to balance the economy, which is shown as "SURPLUS TO BALANCE ECO" (the last entry in the federal budget table), is the federal budget surplus which would result, all other things being held constant, if the necessary personal tax increase were in fact implemented.

All of these variables, the GAP, the necessary personal tax increase, and the surplus to balance the economy, are calculated under the assumption that any projected state and local government surpluses (or deficits) will in fact be realized. In the past, however, the surplus (deficit) of the state and local sector has rarely differed significantly from zero for any substantial length of time (excluding World War II). Thus, the projected GAP and its derivatives will be in error to the extent that any projected surpluses in the state and local sector are assumed not, in fact, to materialize.

The following adjustments will enable the user to account (approximately) for any errors that are due to this source:

1. Allocate any projected state and local surplus or deficit among additional state and local purchases, personal tax relief, and a projected level of the state and local surplus that seems plausible.

2. That portion of the surplus which has been allocated to tax relief should be converted into a change in personal consumption (in current dollars) by means of the following formula (where APC is the average propensity to consume and equals $1.0 - PIR - .001 - S$ as defined earlier in this report):

$$\Delta PCEN = APC / \left\{ 1.0 + [SIBTR + FIBTR] \times APC \right\}.$$

This will account for the leakages in getting from disposable personal income to personal consumption. $\Delta PCEN$ should then be added to both PCE and to the GAP.

3. That portion of the surplus which has been allocated to state and local purchases should be directly added to both state and local purchases and the GAP as given in the product-side table (current dollars).

4. The necessary personal tax increase can then be derived by the following formula, using the revised estimate of the GAP:

$$NPTN = GAPN \text{ (revised)} \times [1.0 + (FIBTR + SIBTR) \times APC] / APC.$$

5. The federal budget surplus necessary to balance the economy can then simply be calculated by added NPTN to the actual federal surplus or deficit as given on the second to last line of the federal budget table.

6. The revised GAP in constant dollars can be derived by following the same steps as those given above, after first deflating by the relevant deflators.

7. That part of the original state and local surplus which is assumed to remain as a surplus will then simply become the projected state and local surplus.

Throughout this procedure, all additions should be made using the algebraic value of the variables concerned. Thus, if the initial GAP, in nominal dollars, is -14.7, and a state and local surplus of 26.1 is allocated entirely to state and local purchases, the revised GAP, in nominal terms, will be 11.4.

Implementation of the AEI Model on Other Computer Systems

Implementation of the AEI model on computer systems other than a DEC-10 system will create minor problems as long as the requirements specified under "General Requirements" are met. Programming changes that are necessary to convert the AEI model for use on other time sharing systems are documented under "Conversions to the AEI Model." In general, these modifications are required in converting the program for batch processing systems as well. The data modifications necessary for batch usage are also explained below.

General Requirements. Since the AEI model is programmed in a higher level version of FORTRAN IV, the computer system employed must possess a FORTRAN processor capable of supporting the following statement types:

(a) double precision statements,

(b) equivalence statements,

(c) namelist statements,

(d) logical if statements.

Each of the above are supported on most large computer systems; however, if (a), (b), or (c) are not supported, the user would be wise to find another computing system, since reprogramming the model to avoid these deficiencies would be extensive. The absence of (d) creates a tedious but less extensive reprogramming problem.

The model requires a minimum storage of 31K (octal). It also requires one peripheral device in addition to a terminal. The program as originally designed employs a disk unit, although the user may elect to substitute a tape unit in the absence of disk devices. This is discussed further in the example modifications set out below. If neither disk nor tape units are available, a card punch could be employed, but this would be rather cumbersome in practice.

Conversions to the AEI Model. Procedures required for conversions to the AEI model are as follows:

1. The first conversion that may be required appears on line 2700 as follows:

        2700   DATA NR, NP/5,5/

Every computer installation has logical unit numbers assigned to each input/output device. All data inputted to the program must be transmitted by some physical input device, such as a terminal, to the computer. Within the program, this input device is referenced by the variable NR which must have a value that corresponds to the logical unit number assigned to the input device. At our installation, a terminal has a logical unit number of 5; therefore, the above statement assigns a value of 5 to NR. A similar situation exists with the output device and the program references it by the variable NP, which the above statement also assigns a value of 5. Since the logical unit numbers assigned to particular I/O devices varies from one installation to another, the statement on line 2700 will, in general, require modification.

2. On time sharing systems other than the DEC-10, the next conversion requirement is the modification of the section of coding reproduced below. The documentation that follows describes its function so that the user may convert it to a form compatible with the computer system he employs:

```
2810            1 CALL LOOKUP (IERR, 'DSET')
2820            IF (IERR) 25, 26, 26
2830            25 CALL IFILE (1, 'DSET')
2840            READ (1) CCCAR, CFR, CIVA71, ...
      .                  .
      .                  .
      .                  .
2920            READ (1) (STRFPA (I), UR(I), ...
2930            END FILE 1
2940            26 PAGE = 0
```

The instruction on line 2810 calls a systems routine which performs a "lookup" under the user's account number for a data file produced by the previous run of the model. If a data file is resident on disk, the program continues execution with the instruction on line 2830; otherwise, execution branches to line 2940. The instruction on line 2830 calls a systems routine which opens the data file as an input file so that it can be accessed by the read instructions beginning at line 2840 and ending at line 2920. At line 2930, all values of the parameters, and exogenous variables from the previous run, have been read from the data file, and this statement closes the file. Program execution then continues with line 2940.

The number "1" appearing on lines 2830 through 2930 is one of the logical unit numbers assigned to disk devices at the computer installation where our program was run. Since this number may not represent a disk device at other installations, the user may have to change it to reflect his installation's assignments.

The set of coding that follows is one modification to the above that should be compatible with most other computer systems. In this example, the number "15" is employed as a logical unit number representing a disk device (or a tape device for batch processing systems that do not support disk devices):

```
 1    REWIND 15
      READ (15, END = 26) DUMMY
      READ (15) CCCAR, CFR, CIVA71, ...
                .
                .
                .
      READ (15, END = 26) (STRFPA (I), UR(I), ...
26    REWIND 15
      PAGE = 0
```

3.   The last section of coding that will require modification appears below and is basically a continuation of the previous section:

```
4710        75   CALL OFILE (1, 'DSET')
4720             WRITE (1) CCCAR, CFR, CIVA71, ...
   .               .
   .               .
   .               .
4800             WRITE (1) (STRFPA (I), UR(I), ...
4810             END FILE 1
```

The instruction on line 4710 calls a systems routine that opens an output data file on disk so that the write instructions on lines 4720 through 4800 can output the current values of the parameters and exogenous variables to the data file. The final instruction on line 4810 closes the data file so that it can be retained until the next run of the model.

Continuing with the example modification presented in 2, the above coding could be replaced with the equivalent set below:

```
DUMMY = 0.0
WRITE (15) DUMMY
WRITE (15) CCCAR, CFR, CIVA71, ...
        .
        .
        .
WRITE (15) (STRFPA(I), UR(I), ...
END FILE 15
```

4.   One final note should be made. Some computer systems do not provide the user with as easy access to tape and disk devices as may have been implied by the example modifications of 2 and 3. Supplementary programming may be required in order to define the specific characteristics of the data file. In any event, the user, unless an experienced programmer, is advised to consult with the systems programmers at his computer installation *before* making the conversions in 2 and 3 above.

Data Modifications for Batch Processing. These modifications are very simple. The user should type one hollerith card, beginning in column one on each card, for each and every response he would have entered via a terminal or teletype. The cards should be arranged in the same order as the responses documented in the user's guide.

Incorporating New Equations in the AEI Model

No write-up can possibly explain how unspecified future equation changes are to be made. At best, it can point out the considerations that a user familiar with FORTRAN IV must keep in mind when making the modification. Program modifications will generally be of two types: changes to an existing equation, and adding an entirely new equation. In the latter case, the new equation must be properly located within the logical structure of the program, and the user can determine this location only by working his way through the program. In either case, the modifications will usually result in adding a new parameter, an exogenous variable, an endogenous variable, or combination of them to the program. To ensure that the program performs properly, these additions must be accounted for within the program. The first two sections below point out each consideration necessary for a proper accounting. This information is followed by a list of the remaining variables in the model.

Modifications Incorporating New Parameters or Exogenous Variables. Each new parameter or exogenous variable must have a variable name by which it is referred to in the program. For illustrative purposes, suppose that we assign it a name of NEWVAR. Then, each item below must be performed:

Item to be Performed	New Parameter Variable	New Exogenous Variable
Append NEWVAR to the dimension statement on line number.	150	220
Append NEWVAR to the NAMELIST statement on line number.	510	560
Add a DATA statement for NEWVAR following line number.	2170	2680
Append NEWVAR to the READ list on line number.	2840	2920
Insert a set of coding similar to that preceding this line number in order to list the NEWVAR.	4150	4670
Modify the FORMAT statement on this line number to adjust the output spacing.	---	4700
Append NEWVAR to the WRITE statement on this line number.	4720	4800

Modifications Incorporating New Endogenous Variables. Each new endogenous variable must also be assigned a variable name and once again suppose that the name is NEWVAR. Each item below should be performed for new endogenous variables:

Item to be Performed	Line Number
Increase the dimension of LAB1 by 1 for *each* NEWVAR that is added.	130
Increase the dimension of X by 10 for *each* NEWVAR that is added.	140
Append *each* NEWVAR to the dimension statement on this line number.	400
Add a comma at the end of this line number and insert additional equivalence expressions for *each* NEWVAR on a newly created line numbered as 985.	980
Add the expression 8HNEWVARΔΔΔ to this line for *each* NEWVAR.	1980
Append a new index number 10 greater than the previous one for *each* NEWVAR.	2070
Add 1 for *each* NEWVAR to the number "13."	2770
Add 1 for each NEWVAR to the number "125" enclosed in parentheses on each of these line numbers.	9910
	10010
	10320

Remaining Variables in the AEI Model.

Variable Name	Description and Function
BR	A branch indicator. When BR=1, execution of the program returns to the input step where the branch was made.
CONVER	Convergence indicator. When CONVER=1, iteration has successfully converged.
C1,C2,etc.	Constants
DIFF	Percentage difference between the previous DPY value and the current DPY value in the iteration block.
IBTR	The ratio of total indirect business taxes to personal consumption expenditures.
ITER	The number of iterations that have been executed.
I, J, K	Increments
NF1,NF2	The number of 8 character groups in the data request message at input step 1, 2, etc.
NYB	Index for the beginning year of the projection output
NYF	Index for the final year of the projection output
OLDDPY	Previous value of DPY in the iteration block.
PITR	PIR + .001, where .001 is the fraction of DPY which is transferred, by consumers to foreigners.
REPLY	A variable for the user's response to the program's data message requests.
RUN	The total number of runs made with the model during any one execution.

Variable Name	Description and Function
SUB1, SUB2	Subsection details in Table 1, Table 2, etc.
SW	Switch indicator. In the beginning of the program, SW=1 indicates that input step 5 is currently being executed. Later in the program, SW=1 indicates that the ALL command has been invoked in step 7.
T, T1	Index for the current point in time during the projection, i.e., a T of 3 means 1973.
TAB1	Title headings for each page of the output.
TAB2	Data request messages.
TEMP	Temporary variable, used for various purposes.
TLAG	Index for the previous point in time during the projection.
TPSOI6	Temporary variable used in the calculation of federal personal taxes and nontaxes.
XIBT	Trial value of IBT less state property taxes used in iteration discussed in Chapter 2.
XPINT	Trial value of PINT used in iteration discussed in Chapter 2.

APPENDIXES

APPENDIX A: ESTIMATING PERSONAL TAX AND NONTAX RECEIPTS

Relationship Between Personal Tax Liability and Receipts. Let TPSOI(t) denote tax liability (statistics of income basis) incurred in year t and TPNIA(t) denote personal income tax receipts (national income and product accounts) in year t.

Tax liability in year t can be broken down into two portions: a withheld portion, W(t), and nonwithheld portion encompassing quarterly installments, final payments and refunds.[52] Thus:

$$TPSOI(t) = W(t) + D_1(t) + D_2(t) + D_3(t) + D_4(t) + FP(t) - R(t) , \qquad (A.1)$$

where:

$W(t)$ = withholding in year t;

$D_1(t)$ = April 15th declarations (installments) in year t, excluding self-employment tax;

$D_2(t)$ = June 15th declarations in year t, excluding self-employment tax;

$D_3(t)$ = September 15th declarations in year t, excluding self-employment tax;

$D_4(t)$ = January 15th declarations in year t+1, excluding self-employment tax (but related to year t liability);

$FP(t)$ = final payment in t+1 on year t liability, excluding self-employment taxes;

$R(t)$ = refunds in t+1 on year t liability.

The subscripts of the terms on the right-hand side of equation (A.1) refer to year of liability. Some of these liabilities will not, however, be received by the Treasury until the year after.

On a receipts basis, taxes received in any year is given by:

$$TPNIA(t) = W(t) + D_1(t) + D_2(t) + D_3(t) + D_4(t-1) + FP(t-1) - R(t-1) \qquad (A.2)$$

(where the subscripts again refer to the year of liability). Subtracting equation (A.1) from equation (A.2) for TPNIA and moving the term TPSOI to the right-hand side yields:

$$TPNIA(t) = TPSOI(t) + [D_4(t-1) - D_4(t)] + [FP(t-1) - R(t-1)] - [FP(t) - R(t)]. \quad (A.3)$$

The last three terms in parentheses on the right-hand side represent the change in net final settlements—reflecting the difference in timing between the two concepts. By estimating the sum of those three terms in equation (A.3) we obtain an adjustment to TPSOI to yield TPNIA. Let ΔFS (change in final settlements) denote the last three terms on the right-hand side of equation (A.3), then equation (A.2) can be written as:

$$TPNIA(t) = TPSOI(t) + FS(t), \text{ and} \quad (A.4)$$

$$\Delta FS(t) = [D_4(t) - D_4(t-1)] + [R(t) - R(t-1)] - [FP(t) - FP(t-1)] . \quad (A.5)$$

Final settlements can be written as a function of the nonwithheld portion of tax liability (TPSOI), and the change in final payments should be a function of the change in nonwithheld tax liability, i.e.

$$\Delta FS = b_0 + b_1 \Delta(TPSOINW), \quad (A.6)$$

where:

$$\Delta TPSOINW = \text{ change in nonwithheld tax liability}$$

$$\Delta TPSOINW = [TPSOI(t) - W(t)] .$$

Equation (A.6) can be rewritten as:

$$\Delta FS = b_0 + b_1 \Delta[TPSOI(t) - W(t)] . \quad (A.6)'$$

Thus, TPNIA can be expressed as:

$$TPNIA(t) = TPSOI(t) + b_0 + b_1 \Delta[TPSOI(t) - W(t)] . \quad (A.4)'$$

Personal Tax Liability (TPSOI). The tax liability equation can be viewed as the product of two variables—the statutory tax rates and the statutory tax base. Under a progressive tax system, this relation should, however, reflect the change in the distribution of the tax base by income class. Thus TPSOI can be expressed as:

$$\Delta TPSOI = \alpha_0 + \alpha_1 \Delta AGI , \quad (A.7)$$

where:

$$\alpha_0 < 0$$

$$\alpha_1 = \text{effective tax rate on AGI}.$$

Since a progressive tax system requires that the change in tax liability rises faster than the change in the tax base—$\frac{\Delta \text{TPSOI}}{\text{TPSOI}} > \frac{\Delta \text{AGI}}{\text{AGI}}$—it follows that equation (A.7) reflects a progressive tax structure if:[53]

$$\alpha_0 < \text{AGI} \left(\alpha_1 - \frac{\text{TPSOI}}{\text{AGI}} \right).$$

To take account of changes in the statutory tax rate, an adjustment factor can be applied to equation (A.7) to yield estimates of tax liability if the tax law changed between (or in each) periods.

Let the factor $(1 + S(t))$ denote a multiplicative factor reflecting a change in the tax code. $S(t)$ represents the percentage change in TPSOI brought about by the change in the tax code. Thus:[54]

$$\text{TPSOI} = \left[\frac{\text{TPSOI}(t-1)}{1 + S(t-1)} + (\alpha_0 + \alpha_1 \, \text{AGI}) \right] [1 + S(t)]. \qquad \text{(A.8)}$$

Since the tax base under the personal income tax differs from personal income, the tax base is related to the taxable portion of personal income as follows:

$$\Delta \text{AGI} = \beta \Delta Y_{PT}, \qquad \text{(A.9)}$$

where:

Y_{PT} = personal income less transfer payments and employee contributions to social security.

Substituting equation (A.9) into (A.8) we get:

$$\text{TPSOI}(t) = \left\{ \frac{\text{TPSOI}(t-1)}{[1 + S(t-1)]} + (\alpha_0 + \alpha_1) \, [\beta \Delta Y_{PT}(t)] \right\} [1 + S(t)]. \qquad \text{(A.10)}$$

Withholding. Withholding $W(t)$ can be expressed as a function of taxable personal income:

$$\Delta W(t) = A_0 + A_1 \, \Delta YPT(t). \qquad \text{(A.11)}$$

89

To allow for changes in the tax code on withholding, we again adjust equation (A.11) by the factor $(1 + SW)$:

$$\Delta W(t) = [A_0 + A_1 \, \Delta YPT(t)] \, [1+SW(t)], \qquad (A.12)$$

where:

$SW(t)$ = change in withholding rate in year t,

$SW(t-1)$ = change in withholding rate in year t-1.

Tax Function for Personal Tax and Nontax Receipts. Personal tax receipts function TP(NIA) can now be derived from previous relationships. By substituting equations (A.10) and (A.12) into equation (A.4)' we get:

$$TPNIA(t) = \frac{TPSOI(t-1)}{[1+S(t-1)]} + [\alpha_0 + \alpha_1 \, \beta \Delta YPT(t)] \, [1+S(t)] + b_0$$

$$+ b_1 \, [\alpha_0 + \alpha_1 \, \beta \Delta YPT(t)] - b_1 \, [A_0 + A_1 \, \Delta YPT(t)] \, [1+SW(t)],$$

or:

$$TPNIA(t) = TPSOI(t-1) \, [1+S(t)] + [1+b_1] \, [\alpha_0 + \alpha_1 \, \beta \Delta YPT(t)] \, [1+S(t)]$$

$$- b_1 \, [A_0 + A_1 \, \Delta YPT(t)] \, [1+SW(t)] + b_0 . \qquad (A.13)$$

Equation (A.13) yields a relationship between personal tax receipts and (1) personal tax liability lagged one period, (2) the change in the taxable portion of personal income, and (3) the current and lagged adjustments for changes in the tax law.

To account for back taxes and nontax receipts, the tax function for personal taxes is modified as follows:

$$TPNIA(t) = TPNIA + \beta_t + NT_t , \qquad (A.14)$$

where:

β_t = back tax as received in year t

NT_t = nontax receipts received in year t.

The variables NT_t and β_t are assumed to be exogenous.

Estimating Personal Tax Liability. TP(SOI) as a function of AGI and AGI as a function of the taxable portion of personal income are both estimated using data for the period 1954-1968. Before TP(SOI) was regressed on AGI, some adjustments were made in the time series for TP(SOI) to allow for changes in the tax laws during the estimation period.[55] The values of TP(SOI) for 1954 through 1963 were multiplied by .81 and by .927 for 1964.

Let TPSOI* denote the adjusted series for TP(SOI):

$$\Delta TPSOI^*(t) = -.936 + .193\ \Delta AGI(t) \tag{A.15}$$
$$(.244)(.009)$$

$$R^2 = .97$$
$$DW = 2.20$$
$$SE = .43.$$

Equation (A.15) gives $\Delta TPSOI$ assuming 1966 law to exist. To reflect the effect of tax law change on liability, equation (A.15) is adjusted by the multiplicative factor $[1 + S(t)]$ or:

$$TPSOI(t) = TPSOI^*(t)\ [1 + S(t)]. \tag{A.16}$$

Solving equation (A.15) for TPSOI*(t) and using the relationship between TPSOI(t) and TPSOI*(t) given in equation (A.16) yields:

$$TP(SOI)_t = \frac{[TPSOI(t-1)]}{[1+S(t-1)]} + [-.936 + .193\ \Delta AGI(t)]\ [1+S(t)], \tag{A.17}$$

or:

$$TPSOI(t) = TPSOI^*(t)\ [1+S(t)]. \tag{A.17}'$$

Expressing AGI as a function of the taxable portion of personal income (YPT), we get using data for the period 1949-1968:

$$\Delta AGI(t) = .868\ \Delta YPT(t) \tag{A.18}$$
$$(.24)$$

$$R^2 = .95$$
$$DW = 2.73$$
$$SE = 2.84.$$

Substituing equation (A.18) into (A.17) yields:

$$TPSOI(t) = \frac{[TPSOI(t-1)]}{[1+S(t-1)]} + [-.936 + (.193)(.868)\Delta YPT(t)]\ [1+S(t)]. \tag{A.19}$$

For example, for 1972, TPSOI* can be written as:

$$TP(SOI)^*_{72} = (-.936) + (.193)(.868)(YPT_{72} - YPT_{71}) + TP(SOI)^*_{71};$$

for 1973:

$$TP(SOI)^*_{73} = (-.936) + (.193)(.868)(YPT_{73} - YPT_{72}) + TP(SOI)^*_{72};$$

or for any year $t \neq t_0$:

$$TP(SOI)^*_{t} = (.936)t + (.193)(.868)[YPT_{t} - YPT_{0}] + TP(SOI)^*_{0}. \qquad \textbf{(A.20)}$$

To allow for exogenous changes in taxes, an "add-on" (CTP) is incorporated in the model, so (A.20) above becomes:

$$TPSOI^*(t) = .936t + (.193)(.868)[YPT(t) - YPT(0)] + TPSOI^*(0) + CTP(t). \qquad \textbf{(A.20)}'$$

APPENDIX B: SOURCE LISTING OF THE AEI MODEL

```
00100          DOUBLE PRECISION DATE,TAB1(7,5),TAB2(16,6)
00110          DOUBLE PRECISION SUB1(14,3),SUB2(17,3),SUB3(24,3),SUB4(12,3)
00120          DOUBLE PRECISION SUB5(8,3),SUB6(8,3)
00130          DOUBLE PRECISION LAB(125),LAB1(13),LABEL,FINISH,ALL,BLNK
00140          REAL    X(1250),IBTR
00150          REAL    CTP(10),DEPA(10),ITC(10),TRC(10),TS(10)
00160          REAL    COLPOP(10),ESPOP(10),FCSIO(10),FECIV(10),FEAF(10),
00170     *            FINT(10),FPRDF(10),FPRO(10),FSUBLS(10),FSURP(10),
00180     *            GPGNPD(10),GRNTS(10),HC(10),HI(10),HS(10),
00190     *            LFT(10),IBT(10),MPT(10),OASDI(10),OTRF(10),PINT(10),
00200     *            POP(10),PRODR(10),SEAO(10),SINT(10),SPCOLB(10),
00210     *            SPESB(10),SPNEB(10),SPRAO(10),SSURPE(10),STPNIA(10),
00220     *            STRFAO(10),STRFPA(10),UR(10),XPT(10)
00230          REAL    BFI(10),BFIN(10),FD(10),FDN(10),FPR(10),FPRDFN(10),
00240     *            FPRN(10),FPRON(10),GAP(10),GAPN(10),GNP(10),GNPN(10),
00250     *            INVI(10),INVIN(10),MPTN(10),NETXM(10),NETXMN(10),NPT(10),
00260     *            NPTN(10),PCE(10),PCEN(10),PDE(10),PDEN(10),PS(10),
00270     *            PSN(10),RCI(10),RCIN(10),SPR(10),SPRB(10),SPRN(10),
00280     *            VATR(10),VATRN(10),XPTN(10)
00290          REAL CCF(10),CCCA(10),CHI(10),CIVA(10),COASDI(10),CP(10),
00300     *            CPCIVA(10),CSI(10),DEFERR(10),DIV(10),DPY(10),ECIV(10),
00310     *            FCSI(10),FCT(10),FFA(10),FGNP58(10),FIBT(10),
00320     *            FTPNIA(10),FTRF(10),GI(10),GNP58(10),GPCEPC(10),
00330     *            GPCEPG(10),GSURP(10),INT(10),LFCIV(10),NCCCA(10),NNP(10),
00340     *            PCEG(10),PCEPC(10),PCEPCG(10),PCER(10),PCERG(10),PCSI(10),
00350     *            PE(10),PERSAV(10),PGNP58(10),PGNPD(10),PGROW(10),PNGR(10),
00360     *            POPWRK(10),PRODIN(10),RGROW(10),SCSI(10),SCT(10),
00370     *            SEB(10),SGNP58(10),SIBT(10),SPT(10),SSURP(10),STRF(10),
00380     *            STRFO(10),SUBLS(10),SURP(10),TOTL3E(10),TOTL3R(10),
00390     *            TOTL5E(10),TOTL5R(10),TOTL6S(10),TPNIA(10),TPSOI(10),
00400     *            TRF(10),TRF3(10),UNDCP(10),YPT(10)
00410          REAL    GNPD(10),PCED(10),RCID(10),PDED(10),PSD(10),FPRD(10),
00420     *            SPRD(10),XPTD(10),MPTD(10)
00430          REAL    GNPD58(10),PCED58(10),RCID58(10),PDED58(10),PSD58(10),
00440     *            FPRD58(10),SPRD58(10),XPTD58(10),MPTD58(10)
00450          REAL    OPS(10,14),OPSN(10,14),FB(10,17),IS(10,24),SLB(10,12),
00460     *            SIB(10,8),PCS(10,8),TITLE(12)
00470          INTEGER REPLY,NO,CO,LO,BR
00480          INTEGER T,T1,TLAG,EDIT,CONVER,PAGE,SW,RUN,INDEX(125)
00490          NAMELIST/PARAM/CCCAR,CFR,CIVA71,COLER,DEPA,EDIT,EPS,FIBTR,
00500     *                  ITC,ITERL,PIR,S,SIBTR,SPTR,TNIA,TRC,TS,
00510     *                  SPRB,CTP
00520          NAMELIST/EXOG/COLPOP,ESPOP,FCSIO,FECIV,FEAF,FINT,FPRDF,FPRO,
00530     *                  FSUBLS,GPGNPD,GRNTS,HC,HI,HS,IBT,LFT,
00540     *                  MPT,OASDI,OTRF,PINT,POP,PRODR,SEAO,SPCOLB,
00550     *                  SPESB,SPNEB,SPRAO,SSURPE,STPNIA,STRFAO,STRFPA,
00560     *                  UR,XPT,CHI,COASDI
00570          EQUIVALENCE (X(1),FINT(1)),(X(11),FSURP(1)),(X(21),IBT(1)),
00580     *(X(31),PINT(1)),(X(41),SPCOLB(1)),(X(51),SPESB(1)),
00590     *(X(61),SPNEB(1)),(X(71),SSURPE(1)),(X(81),STPNIA(1)),
00600     *(X(91),BFI(1)),(X(101),BFIN(1)),(X(111),FD(1)),
00610     *(X(121),FDN(1)),(X(131),FPR(1)),(X(141),FPRDFN(1)),
00620     *(X(151),FPRN(1)),(X(161),FPRON(1)),(X(171),GAP(1)),
00630     *(X(181),GAPN(1)),(X(191),GNP(1)),(X(201),GNPN(1)),
00640     *(X(211),INVI(1)),(X(221),INVIN(1)),(X(231),MPTN(1)),
00650     *(X(241),NETXM(1)),(X(251),NETXMN(1)),(X(261),NPT(1)),
00660     *(X(271),NPTN(1)),(X(281),PCE(1)),(X(291),PCEN(1)),
00670     *(X(301),PDE(1)),(X(311),PDEN(1)),(X(321),PS(1)),
00680     *(X(331),PSN(1)),(X(341),RCI(1)),(X(351),RCIN(1)),
00690     *(X(361),SPR(1)),(X(371),SPRB(1)),(X(381),SPRN(1)),
00700     *(X(391),VATR(1)),(X(401),VATRN(1)),(X(411),XPTN(1))
```

```
00710          EQUIVALENCE (X(421),CCF(1)),(X(431),CCCA(1)),(X(441),CHI(1)),
00720     *(X(451),CIVA(1)),(X(461),COASDI(1)),(X(471),CP(1)),
00730     *(X(481),CPCIVA(1)),(X(491),CSI(1)),(X(501),DEFERR(1)),
00740     *(X(511),DIV(1)),(X(521),DPY(1)),(X(531),ECIV(1)),
00750     *(X(541),FCSI(1)),(X(551),FCT(1)),(X(561),FFA(1)),
00760     *(X(571),FGNP58(1)),(X(581),FIBT(1)),(X(591),FTPNIA(1)),
00770     *(X(601),FTRF(1)),(X(611),GI(1)),(X(621),GNP58(1)),
00780     *(X(631),GPCEPC(1)),(X(641),GPCEPG(1)),(X(651),GSURP(1)),
00790     *(X(661),INT(1)),(X(671),LFCIV(1)),(X(681),NCCCA(1)),
00800     *(X(691),NNP(1)),(X(701),PCEG(1)),(X(711),PCEPC(1)),
00810     *(X(721),PCEPCG(1)),(X(731),PCER(1)),(X(741),PCERG(1)),
00820     *(X(751),PCSI(1)),(X(761),PE(1)),(X(771),PERSAV(1)),
00830     *(X(781),PGNP58(1)),(X(791),PGROW(1)),(X(801),PNGR(1)),
00840     *(X(811),POPWRK(1)),(X(821),PRODIN(1)),(X(831),RGROW(1)),
00850     *(X(841),SCSI(1)),(X(851),SCT(1)),(X(861),SEB(1)),
00860     *(X(871),SGNP58(1)),(X(881),SIBT(1)),(X(891),SPT(1)),
00870     *(X(901),SSURP(1)),(X(911),STRF(1)),(X(921),STRFO(1)),
00880     *(X(931),SUBLS(1)),(X(941),SURP(1)),(X(951),TOTL3E(1)),
00890     *(X(961),TOTL3R(1)),(X(971),TOTL5E(1)),(X(981),TOTL5R(1))
00900          EQUIVALENCE (X(991),TOTL6S(1)),(X(1001),TPNIA(1)),
00910     *(X(1011),TPSOI(1)),(X(1021),TRF(1)),(X(1031),TRF3(1)),
00920     *(X(1041),UNDCP(1)),(X(1051),YPT(1)),(X(1061),FPRD(1)),
00930     *(X(1071),FPRD58(1)),(X(1081),GNPD(1)),(X(1091),GNPD58(1)),
00940     *(X(1101),MPTD(1)),(X(1111),MPTD58(1)),(X(1121),PCED(1)),
00950     *(X(1131),PCED58(1)),(X(1141),PDED(1)),(X(1151),PDED58(1)),
00960     *(X(1161),PGNPD(1)),(X(1171),PSD(1)),(X(1181),PSD58(1)),
00970     *(X(1191),RCID(1)),(X(1201),RCID58(1)),(X(1211),SPRD(1)),
00980     *(X(1221),SPRD58(1)),(X(1231),XPTD(1)),(X(1241),XPTD58(1))
00990          DATA TAB1/8H  *** PR,8H*** PROD,8H** FEDER,8H *** INC,8HSTATE & ,
01000     *          8H  *** S,6H*** PERS,8HODUCT SI,8HUCT SIDE,8HAL BUDGE,
01010     *          8HOME SIDE,8HLOCAL BU,8HAVINGS  ,8HONAL CON,8HDE IN 19,
01020     *          8H IN CURR,8HT IN CUR,8H IN CURR,8HDGET IN ,8HINVESTME,
01030     *          8HSUMPTION,8H71 DOLLA,8HENT DOLL,8HRENT DOL,8HENT DOLL,
01040     *          8HCURRENT ,8HNT BALAN,8H STATIST,8HRS **   ,8HARS  ***,
01050     *          8HLARS **,8HARS ** ,8HDOLLARS ,8HCE *** ,8HICS ****/
01060     DATA TAB2/8HFAMILIAR,8H1. DATE ,8HDATA OK?,8H2. TITLE,8H3. PARAM,
01070     *          8HDATA    ,8H4. EXCG ,8HDATA    ,8H5. END  ,8HDATA    ,
01080     *          8H6. LIST ,8H7. TRACE,8HDATA    ,8HDATA    ,8HYOU MUST,
01090     *          8H8. LAST ,8H WITH PR,8HENTER AS,8H (OK OR ,8H ENTER U,
01100     *          8H LIST AN,8H(SPACE$P,8H LIST AN,8H(SPACE$E,8HOF DATA ,
01110     *          8HENTER ST,8HINPUT DA,8H OF OTHE,8HENTER BE,8HENTER VA,
01120     *          8H ENTER 8,8HRUN (OK ,8HOG? (OK ,8H (99/99/,8HNO)     ,
01130     *          8HP TO 48 ,8HD/OR CHA,8HARAM VN1,8HD/OR CHA,8HXOG VN1=,
01140     *          8HREPEAT S,8HEP NO (1,8HTA (OK 0,8HR ENDOG ,8HGIN YEAR,
01150     *          8HRIABLE N,8H CHARACT,8HOR NO)  ,8HOR NO)  ,8H99)     ,
01160     *          8H       ,8HCHARACTE,8HNGE (LO,,8H=9.9, VN,8HNGE (LO,,
01170     *          8H9.9, VN2,8HTEP? (OK,8H, 2,3, OR,8HR NO)   ,8HVARIABLE,
01180     *          8H/END YEA,8HAME (XXX,8HERS     ,8H       ,8H        ,
01190     *          2*8H              ,
01200     *          8HRS      ,8HCO,LC, 0,8H2=9.9$) ,8HCO,LC, 0,8H=9.9$   ,
01210     *          8H OR NO) ,8H 4)    ,8H       ,8HS (OK OR,8HR (99/99,
01220     *          8HXXXXX)  ,8H      ,8H       ,8H       ,8H       ,
01230     *          2*8H              ,
01240     *          8HR NO)   ,8H      ,8HR NO)   ,8H       ,8H       ,
01250     *          2*8H      ,8H NO)   ,8H)      ,3*8H              /
01260     DATA SUB1/8HGROSS  N,8HCONSUMPT,8HBUSINESS,8HINVENTOR,8HRESIDENT,
01270     *          8HNET EXPO,8HFEDERAL ,8H  DEFENS,8H  OTHER ,8HSTATE & ,
01280     *          8HFINAL DE,8HGAP     ,8HNECESSAR,8HVALUE AD,8HATIONAL ,
01290     *          8HION     ,8H FIXED I,8HY INVEST,8HAL CONST,8HRTS     ,
01300     *          8HPURCHASE,8HE      ,8H       ,8HLOCAL PU,8HMAND    ,
01310     *          8H       ,8HY TAX IN,8HDED RATE,8HPRODUCT ,8H       ,
```

```
01320    *            8HNVEST    ,8HMENT    ,8HRUCTION ,8H        ,8HS       ,
01330    *            8H         ,8H        ,8HRCHASES ,8H        ,8H        ,
01340    *            8HCREASE   /
01350    DATA SUB2/8HPERSONAL,8HCONTRIBU,8HCORPORAT,8HINDIRECT,8H   TOTAL ,
01360    *            8HTOTAL PU,8H  DEFENS,8H   OTHER ,8HTOTAL TR,8H  TO PER,
01370    *            8H  TO FOR,8HGRANTS T,8HSUBSIDIE,8HNET INTE,8H   TOTAL ,
01380    *            8HSURPLUS ,8HSURPLUS ,8H INCOME ,8HTIONS SO,8HE INCOME,
01390    *            8H BUSINES,8HRECIEPTS,8HRCHASES ,8HE        ,8H        ,
01400    *            8HANSFERS ,8HSONS     ,8HEIGNERS ,8HO S&L GO,8HS LESS S,
01410    *            8HREST PAI,8HEXPENDIT,8HOR DEFIC,8HTO BALAN,8HTAX     ,
01420    *            8HCIAL INS,8H TAX    ,8HS TAX   ,8H        ,8H        ,
01430    *        5*8H          ,8HVT'S    ,8HURPLUS  ,8HD        ,8HURES    ,
01440    *            8HIT       ,8HCE ECO, /
01450    DATA SUB3/8HGROSS NA,8H -NON CO,8H -CORP C,8H=NET NAT,8H-CONTRIB,
01460    *            8H  FEDERA,8H   STATE ,8H-CORP PR,8H+SUBSIDI,8H-INDIREC,
01470    *            8H  FEDERA,8H   STATE ,8H+DIVIDEN,8H+NET INT,8H  PERSON,
01480    *            8H  FEDERA,8H   STATE ,8H+TRANSFE,8H  FEDERA,8H   STATE ,
01490    *            8H-PERSONA,8H  FEDERA,8H   STATE ,8H=DISPOSA,8HTIONAL P,
01500    *            8HRP CAPCO,8HAPCONS A,8HIONAL PR,8HUTION SO,8HL       ,
01510    *            8H& LOCAL ,8HOFITS & ,8HES LESS ,8HT BUSINE,8HL       ,
01520    *            8H& LOCAL ,8HDS       ,8HERFST PA,8HAL       ,8HL       ,
01530    *            8H& LOCAL ,8HRS       ,8HL       ,8H& LOCAL ,8HL TAX & ,
01540    *            8HL        ,8H& LOCAL ,8HBLF PERS,8HRODUCT   ,8HN ALLOWS,
01550    *            8HLLOWANCE,8HODUCT    ,8HCIAL INS,8H        ,8H        ,
01560    *            8HIVA      ,8HSURPLUS ,8HSS TAXES,8H        ,8H        ,
01570    *            8H        ,8HID       ,8H        ,8H        ,8H        ,
01580    *        3*8H          ,8H NONTAX ,8H        ,8H        ,8HONAL INC/
01590    DATA SUB4/8H PERSONA,8H+INDIREC,5H+CORPORA,8H+CONTRIB,8H+GRANTS ,
01600    *            8H=TOTAL R,8H PURCHAS,8H+TRANSFE,8H+NET INT,8H-SURPLUS,
01610    *            8H=TOTAL E,8HSURPLUS ,8HL TAX & ,8HT BUSINE,8HTE TAXES,
01620    *            8HUTION SO,8H        ,8HECIEPTS ,8HES       ,8HRS      ,
01630    *            8HERFST PA,8HX OF GOVT,8HXPENDITU,8HOR DEFIC,8H NONTAX ,
01640    *            8HSS TAXES,8H        ,8HCIAL INS,8H        ,8H        ,
01650    *        2*8H          ,8HID       ,8H ENTPR  ,8HRES      ,8HIT(-)   /
01660    DATA SUB5/8H  PERSON,8H  UNDIST,8H  CORPOR,8H  CORP C,8H  NON CO,
01670    *            8HTOTAL SA,8HGOV'T SU,8HGROSS IN,8HAL SAVIN,8H CORP PR,
01680    *            8HATE IVA ,8HAPCONS A,8HRP CAPCO,8HVING     ,8HRPLUS OR,
01690    *            8HVESTMENT,8HG        ,8HOFITS & ,8H        ,8HLLOWANCE,
01700    *            8HN ALLOWS,8H        ,8H DEFICIT,8H        /
01710    DATA SUB6/8HPERSONAL,8HPERCAPIT,8HGROWTH R,8HCONSUMPT,8HPERSONAL,
01720    *            8HPERCAPIT,8HGROWTH R,8HCONSUMPT,8H CONSUMP,8HA CONSUM,
01730    *            8HATE      ,8HION /GNP,8H CONSUMP,8HA CONSUM,8HATE     ,
01740    *            8HION /GNP,8HTION 71$,8HPTIN 71$,8H        ,8H        ,
01750    *            8HTION 71$,8HPTIN 71$,8H        ,8H        /
01760    DATA LAB/8HFINT     ,8HFSURP    ,8HIBT      ,8HPINT     ,8HSPCOLB  ,
01770    *8HSPESB    ,8HSPNEB    ,8HSSURPE   ,8HSTPNIA   ,8HBFI      ,8HBFIN     ,
01780    *8HFD       ,8HFDN      ,8HFPR      ,8HFPRDFN   ,8HFPRN     ,8HFPRON    ,
01790    *8HGAP      ,8HGAPN     ,8HGNP      ,8HGNPN     ,8HINVI     ,8HINVIN    ,
01800    *8HMPTN     ,8HNETXM    ,8HNETXMN   ,8HNPT      ,8HNPTN     ,8HPCE      ,
01810    *8HPCEN     ,8HPDE      ,8HPDEN     ,8HPS       ,8HPSN      ,8HRCI      ,
01820    *8HRCIN     ,8HSPR      ,8HSPRB     ,8HSPRN     ,8HVATR     ,8HVATRN    ,
01830    *8HXPTN     ,8HCCF      ,8HCCCA     ,8HCHI      ,8HCIVA     ,8HCOASDI   ,
01840    *8HCP       ,8HCPCIVA   ,8HCSI      ,8HDEFERR   ,8HDIV      ,8HDPY      ,
01850    *8HECIV     ,8HFCSI     ,8HFCT      ,8HFFA      ,8HFGNP58   ,8HFIBT     ,
01860    *8HFTPNIA   ,8HFTRF     ,8HGI       ,8HGNP58    ,8HGPCEPC   ,8HGPCEPG   ,
01870    *8HGSURP    ,8HINT      ,8HLFCIV    ,8HNCCCA    ,8HNNP      ,8HPCEG     ,
01880    *8HPCEPC    ,8HPCEPCG   ,8HPCER     ,8HPCERG    ,8HPCSI     ,8HPE       ,
01890    *8HPERSAV   ,8HPGNP58   ,8HPGROW    ,8HPNGR     ,8HPOPWRK   ,8HPRODIN   ,
01900    *8HRGROW    ,8HSCSI     ,8HSCT      ,8HSEB      ,8HSGNP58   ,8HSIBT     ,
01910    *8HSPT      ,8HSSURP    ,8HSTRF     ,8HSTRFO    ,8HSUBLS    ,8HSURP     ,
01920    *8HTOTL3E   ,8HTOTL3R   ,8HTOTL5E   ,8HTOTL5R   ,8HTOTL6S   ,8HTPNIA    ,
```

95

```
01930        *8HTPSOI    ,8HTRF     ,8HTRF3    ,8HUNDCP   ,8HYPT     ,8HFPRD    ,
01940        *8HFPRD58   ,8HGNPD    ,8HGNPD58  ,8HMPTD    ,8HMPTD58  ,
01950        *13*8H     /
01960         DATA LAB1/8HPCED    ,8HPCED58  ,8HPDED    ,
01970        *8HPDED58   ,8HPGNPD   ,8HPSD     ,8HPSD58   ,8HRCID    ,8HRCID58  ,
01980        *8HSPRD     ,8HSPRD58  ,8HXPTD    ,8HXPTD58  /
01990         DATA INDEX/1,11,21,31,41,51,61,71,81,91,101,111,121,131,141,
02000        *151,161,171,181,191,201,211,221,231,241,251,261,271,281,291,
02010        *301,311,321,331,341,351,361,371,381,391,401,411,421,431,
02020        *441,451,461,471,481,491,501,511,521,531,541,551,561,571,581,
02030        *591,601,611,621,631,641,651,661,671,681,691,701,711,721,731,
02040        *741,751,761,771,781,791,801,811,821,831,841,851,861,871,
02050        *881,891,901,911,921,931,941,951,961,971,981,991,1001,1011,
02060        *1021,1031,1041,1051,1061,1071,1081,1091,1101,1111,1121,1131,1141,
02070        *1151,1161,1171,1181,1191,1201,1211,1221,1231,1241/
02080         DATA CCCAR,CFR,CIVA71,EDIT,EPS,FIBTR/0,356,0,16,-4,7,0,0,001,
02090        *0,0280/
02100         DATA COLER,ITERL,PIR,S,SIBTR,SPTR/0,81,10,0,025,0,07,0,062,
02110        *0,038/
02120         DATA TNIA/0,059/,CTP/4*0,0,6*-0,40/,ITC/10*1,0/
02130         DATA TS/10*0,93/
02140         DATA DEPA/0,01,0,018,0,0238,0,0259,0,0293,0,0293,0,0254,
02150        *0,022,0,0199,0,0179/
02160         DATA TRC/0,424,0,410,0,400,0,415,0,394,0,394,0,393,0,392,
02170        *0,391,0,391/
02180         DATA CHI/10*0,0/
02190         DATA COASDI/38,,44,,50,6,73,9,79,8,85,8,91,6,101,9,109,1,117,2/
02200         DATA COLPOP/7796,,8119,,8449,,8792,,9147,,9457,,9710,,9930,,
02210        *          10125,,10284,/
02220         DATA ESPOP/50827,,50415,,49994,,49538,,49009,,48621,,48323,,
02230        *          48107,,47972,,47968,/
02240         DATA FCSIO/9,9,10,9,11,9,12,8,13,5,14,6,15,5,16,7,17,9,
02250        *18,9/
02260         DATA FECIV/2*2000,,2020,,2017,,2030,,2000,,2030,,2050,,2070,,
02270        * 2100,/
02280         DATA FEAF/2*2490,,2396,,2300,,2200,,5*2100,/
02290         DATA FINT/14,3,14,7,15,1,15,5,15,5,15,2,14,9,14,6,14,3,13,9/
02300         DATA FPRDF/2*75,,74,,73,,69,4,70,4,71,4,71,0,69,5,69,2/
02310         DATA FPRO/23,,21,4,25,,26,,37,1,36,0,36,3,37,2,38,1,38,9/
02320         DATA FSUBLS/5,2,5,6,6,0,6,6,5,9,6,1,6,0,3*5,9/
02330         DATA GNP/1749,1,9*0,0/
02340         DATA GNPD/1,0,9*0,0/
02350         DATA GPGNPD/0,0,0,026,8*0,025/
02360         DATA GRNTS/29,,32,,36,,40,,44,5,46,7,49,6,52,,54,6,57,4/
02370         DATA HC/10*15,53/
02380         DATA HI/10*0,0/
02390         DATA HS/2,1,2,0,2,1,2,2,2,3,2,3,2,4,2,4,2,5,2,5/
02400         DATA IBT/72,7,9*0,0/
02410         DATA LFT/86900,,88100,,90000,,91800,,93300,,94900,,96600,,
02420        *98200,,99800,,101400,/
02430         DATA MPT/10*0,0/
02440         DATA OASDI/70,,82,,95,,108,,113,5,122,4,130,9,140,5,151,,162,3/
02450         DATA OTRF/10*0,0/
02460         DATA PCEPC/3199,0,9*0,0/
02470         DATA PCEPCG/3199,0,9*0,0/
02480         DATA PGNPD/1,0,9*0,0/
02490         DATA PINT/17,6,9*0,0/
02500         DATA POP/206886,,209016,,211195,,213424,,215703,,218301,,
02510        *          220407,,222828,,225282,,227765,/
02520         DATA POPWRK/986,6,9*0,0/
02530         DATA PRODR/0,0,0,042,0,04,0,035,6*0,03/
```

```
02540          DATA PRODIN/1,0,9*0,0/
02550          DATA SEAO/10*0,0/
02560          DATA SINT/10*0,4/
02570          DATA SPCOLB/12,0,9*0,0/
02580          DATA SPESB/42,6,9*0,0/
02590          DATA SPNEB/80,8,9*0,0/
02600          DATA SPRAO/10*0,0/
02610          DATA SPRB/135,4,9*0,0/
02620          DATA SSURPE/4,1,9*0,0/
02630          DATA STPNIA/27,4,9*0,0/
02640          DATA STRFAO/4*0,0,6*0,0/
02650          DATA STRFPA/9,3,10,2,11,2,12,3,9,0,9,8,10,5,11,1,11,8,12,4/
02660          DATA UR/0,06,0,056,0,046,0,040,6*0,040/
02670          DATA XPT/10*0,0/
02680          DATA SPT/10*0,0/
02690          DATA NO,CO,LO,RUN,SAVE/4HNO  ,4HCO  ,4HLO  ,0,0,0/
02700          DATA NR,NP/5,5/
02710          DATA BLNK,FINISH,ALL/8H        ,8HFINISH  ,8HALL     /
02720   C      -------------------------------------------------------------
02730   C      ******INPUT SECTION
02740   C      -------------------------------------------------------------
02750          WRITE(NP,900)
02760     900 FORMAT(1X,28HLRBP MODEL  VERSION 03/24/73)
02770          DO 9 I=1,13
02780          J=112+I
02790          LAB(J)=LAB1(I)
02800       9 CONTINUE
02810       1 CALL LOOKUP(IERR,'DSET')
02820          IF(IERR)25,26,26
02830      25 CALL IFILE(1,'DSET')
02840          READ(1) CCCAR,CFR,CIVA71,COLER,EDIT,EPS,SIBTR,FIBTR,ITERL,PIR,S,SIBTR
02850        * SPTR,TNIA,(CTP(I),DEPA(I),ITC(I),TRC(I),TS(I),SPRB(I),I=1,10)
02860          READ(1) (COLPOP(I),ESPOP(I),FCSIO(I),FECIV(I),FEAF(I),I=1,10)
02870          READ(1) (FINT(I),FPRDF(I),FPRO(I),FSUBLS(I),FSURP(I),I=1,10)
02880          READ(1) (GPGNPD(I),GRNTS(I),HC(I),HI(I),HS(I),IBT(I),I=1,10)
02890          READ(1) (LFT(I),MPT(I),OASDI(I),OTRF(I),PINT(I),POP(I),I=1,10)
02900          READ(1) (PRODR(I),SEAO(I),SPCOLB(I),SPESB(I),SPNEB(I),I=1,10)
02910          READ(1) (SPRAO(I),SSURPE(I),STPNIA(I),STRFAO(I),I=1,10)
02920          READ(1) (STRFPA(I),UR(I),XPT(I),CHI(I),COASDI(I),I=1,10)
02930          END FILE 1
02940      26 PAGE=0
02950          NF1=3
02960          NF2=4
02970          NF3=5
02980          NF4=6
02990          NYB=5
03000          NYF=10
03010          SW=0
03020          BR=0
03030          DO 2 I=1,6
03040          TITLE(I)=BLNK
03050       2 CONTINUE
03060          DO 4 I=2,9
03070          DO 4 J=2,10
03080          K=J+(I-1)*10
03090          X(K)=0,0
03100       4 CONTINUE
03110          DO 15 I=2,10
03120          SPRB(I)=0,0
03130      15 CONTINUE
03140          WRITE(NP,5) (TAB2(1,I),I=1,NF2)
```

```
03150        WRITE(NP,3)
03160      3 FORMAT(1H0)
03170      5 FORMAT(1X,6A8,/)
03180        READ(NR,6) REPLY
03190      6 FORMAT(1A2)
03200        IF(REPLY .EQ. NO)GO TO 10
03210        NF1=1
03220        NF2=1
03230        NF3=1
03240        NF4=1
03250     10 IF(RUN ,NE. 0)GO TO 20
03260     11 WRITE(NP,5) (TAB2(2,I),I=1,NF2)
03270        WRITE(NP,3)
03280        READ(NR,12) DATE
03290     12 FORMAT(1A8)
03300        WRITE(NP,5) (TAB2(3,I),I=1,NF1)
03310        WRITE(NP,3)
03320        READ(NR,6) REPLY
03330        IF(REPLY .EQ. NO)GO TO 11
03340        IF(SW ,NE. 0)GO TO 50
03350     20 WRITE(NP,5) (TAB2(4,I),I=1,NF3)
03360        WRITE(NP,3)
03370        READ(NR,22) TITLE
03380     22 FORMAT(12A4)
03390        WRITE(NP,5) (TAB2(3,I),I=1,NF1)
03400        WRITE(NP,3)
03410        READ(NR,6) REPLY
03420        IF(REPLY .EQ. NO)GO TO 20
03430        IF(SW ,NE. 0)GO TO 50
03440     30 WRITE(NP,5) (TAB2(5,I),I=1,NF4)
03450        WRITE(NP,3)
03460        READ(NR,6) REPLY
03470        IF(REPLY .EQ. NO)GO TO 40
03480        IF(REPLY .EQ. CO)GO TO 31
03490        BR=1
03500        GO TO 298
03510     33 BR=0
03520        IF(REPLY .EQ. LO)GO TO 30
03530     31 WRITE(NP,5) (TAB2(6,I),I=1,NF3)
03540        WRITE(NP,3)
03550        READ(NR,PARAM)
03560        WRITE(NP,5) (TAB2(3,I),I=1,NF1)
03570        WRITE(NP,3)
03580        READ(NR,6) REPLY
03590        IF(REPLY .EQ. NO)GO TO 31
03600        IF(SW ,NE. 0)GO TO 50
03610     40 WRITE(NP,5) (TAB2(7,I),I=1,NF4)
03620        WRITE(NP,3)
03630        READ(NR,6) REPLY
03640        IF(REPLY .EQ. NO)GO TO 50
03650        IF(REPLY .EQ. CO)GO TO 41
03660        BR=1
03670        GO TO 299
03680     43 BR=0
03690        IF(REPLY .EQ. LO)GO TO 40
03700     41 WRITE(NP,5) (TAB2(8,I),I=1,NF3)
03710        WRITE(NP,3)
03720        READ(NR,EXOG)
03730        WRITE(NP,5) (TAB2(3,I),I=1,NF1)
03740        WRITE(NP,3)
03750        READ(NR,6) REPLY
```

```
03760          IF(REPLY .EQ. NO)GO TO 41
03770       50 WRITE(NP,5) (TAB2(9,I),I=1,NF3)
03780          WRITE(NP,3)
03790          READ(NR,6) REPLY
03800          IF(REPLY .EQ. NO)GO TO 60
03810          WRITE(NP,5) (TAB2(10,I),I=1,NF3)
03820          WRITE(NP,3)
03830          READ(NR,51) I
03840       51 FORMAT(I1)
03850          SW=1
03860          GO TO(10,20,30,40),I
03870       60 WRITE(NP,5) (TAB2(11,I),I=1,NF2)
03880          WRITE(NP,3)
03890          READ(NR,6) REPLY
03900          IF(REPLY .EQ. NO)GO TO 75
03910          PAGE=PAGE+1
03920          WRITE(NP,200) TITLE,DATE,PAGE
03930      298 WRITE(NP,301)
03940      301 FORMAT(24X,25HINITIAL VALUES PARAM LIST,//
03950         *1X,12H--CCCAR---,1X,10H---CFR----,1X,10H--CIVA71--,1X,
03960         *12H---COLER--,1X,12H---EDIT---,1X,12H---FPS----)
03970          TEMP=EDIT
03980          WRITE(NP,320) CCCAR,CFR,CIVA71,COLER,TEMP,FPS
03990          WRITE(NP,302)
04000      302 FORMAT(1H0,1X,12H---FIBTR--,1X,12H---ITERL--,
04010         *1X,12H---PIR----,1X,10H-----S----,1X,12H---SIBTR--)
04020          TEMP=ITERL
04030          WRITE(NP,320) FIBTR,TEMP,PIR,S,SIBTR
04040          WRITE(NP,303)
04050      303 FORMAT(1H0,1X,12H---SPTR---,1X,12H----TNIA---)
04060          WRITE(NP,320) SPTR,TNIA
04070      320 FORMAT(1X,6(F10.5,1X))
04080          WRITE(NP,324)
04090      304 FORMAT(1H0,  2HYR,1X,12H----CTP---,1X,12H---DEPA---,1X,
04100         *10H---ITC----,1X,12H---SPRB---,1X,10H---TRC----,1X,10H-----TS----)
04110          DO 306 I=1,12
04120          J=I+70
04130          WRITE(NP,325) J,CTP(I),DEPA(I),ITC(I),SPRB(I),TRC(I),TS(I)
04140      325 FORMAT(1X,I2,1X,6(F10.3,1X))
04150      306 CONTINUE
04160          IF(BR .EQ. 1)GO TO 33
04170      299 WRITE(NP,307)
04180      307 FORMAT(///24X,25HINITIAL VALUES EXOG  LIST,//
04190         *1X,2HYR,1X,12H---CHI----,1X,12H--COASDI--,1X,12H--COLPOP--,
04200         *1X,12H--ESPOP---,1X,12H--FCSIO---,1X,12H---FECIV--)
04210          DO 328 I=1,12
04220          J=I+70
04230          WRITE(NP,325) J,CHI(I),COASDI(I),COLPOP(I),ESPOP(I),FCSIO(I),
04240         *FECIV(I)
04250      328 CONTINUE
04260          WRITE(NP,329)
04270      309 FORMAT(1H0,  2HYR,1X,12H---FEAF---,1X,12H---FINT---,1X,
04280         *12H--FPRDF---,1X,12H---FPRO---,1X,12H--FSURLS--,1X,12H--GPGNPD--)
04290          DO 310 I=1,12
04300          J=I+70
04310          WRITE(NP,325) J,FEAF(I),FINT(I),FPRDF(I),FPRO(I),FSURLS(I),
04320         *GPGNPD(I)
04330      310 CONTINUE
04340          WRITE(NP,311)
04350      311 FORMAT(1H0,  2HYR,1X,12H--GRNTS---,1X,12H-----HC----,1X,
04360         *12H----HI----,1X,12H----HS----,1X,12H----IBT----,1X,12H---LFT----)
```

```
04370        DO 312 I=1,12
04380        J=I+70
04390        WRITE(NP,325) J,GRNTS(I),HC(I),HI(I),HS(I),IBT(I),LFT(I)
04400    312 CONTINUE
04410        IF(BR .EQ. 1)GO TO 320
04420        PAGE=PAGE+1
04430        WRITE(NP,200) TITLE,DATE,PAGE
04440    320 WRITE(NP,313)
04450    313 FORMAT(1H0,   2HYR,1X,10H---MPT----,1X,10H--OASDI---,1X,
04460       *10H---OTRF---,1X,10H---PINT---,1X,10H---POP----,1X,10H--PRODR---)
04470        DO 314 I=1,12
04480        J=I+70
04490        WRITE(NP,325) J,MPT(I),OASDI(I),OTRF(I),PINT(I),POP(I),
04500       *PRODR(I)
04510    314 CONTINUE
04520        WRITE(NP,315)
04530    315 FORMAT(1H0,   2HYR,1X,10H---SEAO---,1X,10H---SINT---,1X,
04540       *10H--SPCOLB--,1X,10H--SPESR---,1X,10H--SPNEB---,1X,10H--SPRAO---)
04550        DO 316 I=1,12
04560        J=I+70
04570        WRITE(NP,325) J,SEAO(I),SINT(I),SPCOLB(I),SPESR(I),SPNEB(I),
04580       *SPRAO(I)
04590    316 CONTINUE
04600        WRITE(NP,317)
04610    317 FORMAT(1H0,   2HYR,1X,10H--SSURPE--,1X,10H--STPNIA--,1X,
04620       *10H--STRFAO--,1X,10H--STRFPA--,1X,10H----UR----,1X,10H---XPT----)
04630        DO 318 I=1,12
04640        J=I+70
04650        WRITE(NP,325) J,SSURPE(I),STPNIA(I),STRFAO(I),STRFPA(I),UR(I),
04660       *XPT(I)
04670    318 CONTINUE
04680        IF(BR .EQ. 1)GO TO 43
04690        WRITE(NP,21)
04700     21 FORMAT(1X,26(/),1X,71(1H-))
04710     75 CALL OFILE(1,'OSET')
04720        WRITE(1) CCCAR,CFR,CIVA71,COLER,EDIT,EPS,SIBTR,FIBTR,ITERL,PIR,S,SIBTR
04730       * SFTR,TNIA,(CTP(I),DEPA(I),ITC(I),THC(I),TS(I),SPRB(I),I=1,12)
04740        WRITE(1) (COLPOP(I),ESPOP(I),FCSIO(I),FECIV(I),FFAF(I),I=1,12)
04750        WRITE(1) (FINT(I),FPRDF(I),FPRO(I),FSURLS(I),FSURP(I),I=1,12)
04760        WRITE(1) (GPGNPD(I),GRNTS(I),HC(I),HI(I),HS(I),IBT(I),I=1,12)
04770        WRITE(1) (LFT(I),MPT(I),OASDI(I),OTRF(I),PINT(I),POP(I),I=1,12)
04780        WRITE(1) (PRODR(I),SEAO(I),SPCOLB(I),SPESR(I),SPNEB(I),I=1,12)
04790        WRITE(1) (SPRAO(I),SSURPE(I),STPNIA(I),STRFAO(I),I=1,12)
04800        WRITE(1) (STRFPA(I),UR(I),XPT(I),CHI(I),COASDI(I),I=1,12)
04810        END FILE 1
04820        WRITE(NP,76)
04830     76 FORMAT(1X,10HRUNNING---,///)
04840        C4=SPESR(1)/50807.0
04850        C5=SPCOLB(1)/7896.0
04860        C6=SPNEB(1)/206886.0
04870        DO 110 T1=1,12
04880    C    ------------------------------------------------------------------
04890    C    *****CALCULATE GNP PATH
04900    C    ------------------------------------------------------------------
04910        IF(T1 .EQ. 1)GO TO 100
04920        LFT(T1)=LFT(T1)*(1.0+2.0*(0.04-UR(T1)))
04930        LFCIV(T1)=LFT(T1)-FEAF(T1)
04940        ECIV(T1)=(1.0-UR(T1))*LFCIV(T1)
04950        SPESR(T1) = (C4*(1.024**(T1-1)))*ESPOP(T1)
04960        SPCOLB(T1) = (C5*(1.029**(T1-1)))*COLPOP(T1)
04970        SPNEB(T1) = (C6*(1.035**(T1-1)))*POP(T1)
```

```
04980            SPRB(T1)=SPESB(T1)+SPCOLB(T1)+SPNEB(T1)
04990            SEB(T1)=(SPESB(T1)/SPESB(1))*4142.0+(SPCOLB(T1)/SPCOLB(1))*1339.0
05000           *+(SPNEB(T1)/SPNEB(1))*4461.0
05010            PE(T1)=ECIV(T1)-SEB(T1)-FECIV(T1)-SEAO(T1)
05020            POPWRK(T1)=POPWRK(T1-1)*(1.0+PRODR(T1))
05030            PGNP58(T1)=(PE(T1)*POPWRK(T1))/1.0E+05
05040            SGNP58(T1)=(SEB(T1)+SEAO(T1))*0.003915
05050            FGNP58(T1)=(FEAF(T1)+FECIV(T1))*0.004749
05060            GNP58(T1)=PGNP58(T1)+FGNP58(T1)+SGNP58(T1)
05070            GNP(T1)=GNP58(T1)*1.416
05080            PNGR(T1)=PGNP58(T1)/GNP58(T1)
05090            PRODIN(T1)=(1.0+PRODR(T1))*PRODIN(T1-1)
05100            PGNPD(T1)=(1.0+GPGNPD(T1))*PGNPD(T1-1)
05110            GNPN(T1)=1.360*PGNP58(T1)*PGNPD(T1)+(FGNP58(T1)+SGNP58(T1))
05120           **2.028*(PRODIN(T1)*PGNPD(T1))
05130            GNPD(T1)=GNPN(T1)/GNP(T1)
05140            GNPD58(T1)=GNPN(T1)/GNP58(T1)
05150            RGROW(T1)=(GNP(T1)/GNP(T1-1))-1.0
05160            PGROW(T1)=(GNPD(T1)/GNPD(T1-1))-1.0
05170            GO TO 105
05180     C      ------------------------------------------------------
05190     C      ******DEFLATOR BLOCK
05200     C      ------------------------------------------------------
05210     100  GNPD58(T1)=1.416
05220     105  PCED58(T1)= .177+0.824*GNPD58(T1)
05230            RCID58(T1)=-.154+1.172*GNPD58(T1)
05240            PDED58(T1)= .283+0.687*GNPD58(T1)
05250            PSD58(T1)= -.510+1.507*GNPD58(T1)
05260            FPRD58(T1)=-.363+1.353*GNPD58(T1)
05270            SPRD58(T1)=-.774+1.780*GNPD58(T1)
05280            XPTD58(T1)= .419+0.573*GNPD58(T1)
05290            MPTD58(T1)= .578+4.290*GNPD58(T1)
05300     110  CONTINUE
05310            DO 115 T1=1,10
05320            PCED(T1)=PCED58(T1)/1.346
05330            RCID(T1)=RCID58(T1)/1.502
05340            PDED(T1)=PDED58(T1)/1.241
05350            PSD(T1)=PSD58(T1)/1.704
05360            FPRD(T1)=FPRD58(T1)/1.568
05370            SPRD(T1)=SPRD58(T1)/1.759
05380            XPTD(T1) = XPTD58(T1)/1.258
05390            MPTD(T1) = MPTD58(T1)/1.245
05400     115  CONTINUE
05410     C      ------------------------------------------------------------------
05420     C      ****** INITIAL CALCULATIONS
05430     C      ------------------------------------------------------------------
05440            PITR=PIR+0.001
05450            IBTR=SIBTR+FIBTR
05460            C1=0.193*0.868
05470            C2=1.0+TNIA
05480            C3=1.0-S-PITR
05490            C7=1.0+IBTR*C3
05500            NCCCA(1)=0.032*GNPN(1)
05510            DIV(1)=0.0272*GNPN(1)
05520     C      ------------------------------------------------------------------
05530     C      ******BEGIN SIMULATION
05540     C      ------------------------------------------------------------------
05550            DO 195 T=2,10
05560            TLAG=T-1
05570            R=0.03+PGROW(T)
05580            G3=1.0+PGROW(T)+RGROW(T)
```

```
05590          G5=RGROW(T)+PGROW(T)
05600    C      --------------------------------------------------------------
05610    C      ******PRODUCT SIDE BLOCK
05620    C      --------------------------------------------------------------
05630          INVI(T)=0.012*PNGR(T)*GNP(T)
05640          RCI(T)=HS(T)*HC(T)*RCID58(1)
05650          NETXM(T)=XPT(T)-MPT(T)
05660          SPR(T)=SPRB(T)+SPRAO(T)
05670          FPR(T)=FPRDF(T)+FPRO(T)
05680          PS(T)=PNGR(T)*GNP(T)*0.0374
05690          PDE(T)=PNGR(T)*GNP(T)*0.0866
05700          BFI(T)=PS(T)+PDE(T)
05710    C      --------------------------------------------------------------
05720    C      ******INCOME SIDE BLOCK
05730    C      --------------------------------------------------------------
05740          NCCCA(T)=1.19+0.009696*GNPN(T)+0.6995*NCCCA(TLAG)
05750          CCF(T)=CFR*GNPN(T)
05760          FCSI(T)=COASDI(T)+CHI(T)+FCSIO(T)
05770          SCSI(T)=0.068*SPR(T)*SPRD(T)
05780          CSI(T)=FCSI(T)+SCSI(T)
05790          SSURPE(T)=SSURPE(1)*(EXP((ALOG(GNPN(T)/1049.1))/TLAG))**TLAG
05800          SURLS(T)=FSURLS(T)-SSURPE(T)
05810          DIV(T)=0.07925*CCF(T)+0.599*DIV(TLAG)
05820          STRFO(T)=SCSI(T)*0.69
05830          STRF(T)=STRFPA(T)+STRFAO(T)+STRFO(T)
05840          FFA(T)=2.5*G3**TLAG
05850          FTRF(T)=OASDI(T)+HI(T)+OTRF(T)-FFA(T)
05860          TRF3(T)=FTRF(T)+FFA(T)
05870          TRF(T)=FTRF(T)+STRF(T)
05880    C      --------------------------------------------------------------
05890    C      ******ITTERRATIVE BLOCK
05900    C      --------------------------------------------------------------
05910          SPT(T)=SPTR*GNPN(T)
05920          XIBT=(IBT(TLAG)-SPT(TLAG))*G3
05930          XPINT=PINT(TLAG)*G3
05940          TEMP=GNPN(T)-NCCCA(T)-CCF(T)+DIV(T)+FINT(T)+SINT(T)-CSI(T)+
05950         *FSUBLS(T)-SSURPE(T)-SPT(T)
05960          PCSI(T)=0.486*CSI(T)
05970          STPNIA(T)=STPNIA(1)*(1.0+(1.7*((EXP((ALOG(GNPN(T)/1049.1))/
05980         *TLAG))-1.0)))**TLAG
05990          IF(EDIT .EQ. 0)GO TO 125
06000          J=70+T
06010          WRITE(NP,120) J,TEMP,PCSI(T),STPNIA(T),TRF(T)
06020      120 FORMAT(5X,22H******ITTERRATION BLOCK,2X,5HYEAR ,I2,
06030         */5X,6HTEMP  ,2X,6HPCSI  ,2X,6HSTPNIA,2X,6HTRF   ,
06040         */5X,4(F6.1,2X),
06050         *//2X,4HITER,2X,6HXIBT  ,2X,6HXPINT ,2X,6HYPT   ,2X,6HTPSOI6,2X,
06060         *6HTPSOI ,2X,6HFTPNIA,2X,6HDPY   ,2X,6HDIFF  )
06070      125 ITER=1
06080          DIFF=1.0
06090          CONVER=0
06100          OLDDPY=0.0
06110      130 YPT(T)=TEMP+PCSI(T)-XIBT+XPINT
06120          TPSOI6=-0.936*(T+2)+C1*(YPT(T)-655.6)+70.3
06130          TPSOI(T)=TPSOI6*TS(T)+CTP(T)
06140          FTPNIA(T)=TPSOI(T)*C2
06150          DPY(T)=YPT(T)+TRF(T)-PCSI(T)-FTPNIA(T)-STPNIA(T)
06160          IF(ITER .EQ. 1)GO TO 135
06170          DIFF=(DPY(T)-OLDDPY)/OLDDPY
06180          IF(ABS(DIFF) .LE. EPS)CONVER=1
06190      135 OLDDPY=DPY(T)
```

102

```
06200              IF(EDIT .EQ. 0)GO TO 145
06210              WRITE(NP,140) ITER,XIBT,XPINT,YPT(T),TPSOI6,TPSOI(T),FTPNIA(T),
06220             *DPY(T),DIFF
06230        140 FORMAT(4X,I2,2X,7(F6.1,2X),F6.3)
06240        145 PCEN(T)=C3*DPY(T)
06250              XPINT=PIR*DPY(T)
06260              SIBT(T)=SIBTR*PCEN(T)
06270              FIBT(T)=FIBTR*PCEN(T)
06280              XIBT=SIBT(T)+FIBT(T)
06290              IF(CONVER .EQ. 1)GO TO 150
06300              IF(ITER .GE. ITERL)GO TO 155
06310              ITER=ITER+1
06320              GO TO 130
06330        150 IBT(T)=XIBT+SPT(T)
06340              PINT(T)=XPINT
06350              SIBT(T)=SIBT(T)+SPT(T)
06360              INT(T)=FINT(T)+SINT(T)+PINT(T)
06370              PERSAV(T)=S*DPY(T)
06380              GO TO 160
06390        155 NYF=TLAG
06400              NYB=NYF-5
06410              IF(NYB .LT. 1)NYB=1
06420              GO TO 199
06430     C    ---------------------------------------------------------------
06440     C    ******LAST EQUATION PRODUCT SIDE BLOCK
06450     C    ---------------------------------------------------------------
06460        160 PCE(T)=PCEN(T)/PCED(T)
06470     C    ---------------------------------------------------------------
06480     C    ******FINAL ACCOUNTING BLOCK
06490     C    ---------------------------------------------------------------
06500              INVIN(T) = INVI(T)*PGNPD(T)
06510              RCIN(T)=RCI(T)*RCID(T)
06520              PCEN(T)=PCE(T)*PCED(T)
06530              PDEN(T)=PDE(T)*PDED(T)
06540              PSN(T)=PS(T)*PSD(T)
06550              BFIN(T)=PSN(T)+PDEN(T)
06560              XPTN(T) = XPT(T)*XPTD(T)
06570              MPTN(T) = MPT(T)*MPTD(T)
06580              SPRN(T)=((0.7*SPESB(T)+COLER*SPCOLB(T)+0.44*(SPNEB(T)+SPRAO(T)))
06590             **PRODIN(T)+0.3*SPESB(T)+(1.0-COLER)*SPCOLB(T)+0.54*(SPNEB(T)
06600             *+SPRAO(T)))*PGNPD(T)
06610              SPRD(T)=SPRN(T)/SPR(T)
06620              FPRDFN(T)=FPRDF(T)*FPRD(T)
06630              FPRON(T)=FPRO(T)*FPRD(T)
06640              FPRN(T)=FPR(T)*FPRD(T)
06650              NETXMN(T)=NETXM(T)
06660              FD(T)=PCE(T)+BFI(T)+INVI(T)+RCI(T)+NETXM(T)+FPR(T)+SPR(T)
06670              TEMP=PCEN(T)+BFIN(T)+INVIN(T)+RCIN(T)+NETXMN(T)+FPRN(T)+SPRN(T)
06680              GAP(T)=FD(T)-GNP(T)
06690              GAPN(T)=GAP(T)*GNPD(T)
06700              FDN(T)=FD(T)*GNPD(T)
06710              DEFERR(T)=FDN(T)/TEMP
06720     C    ---------------------------------------------------------------
06730     C    ******ADJUST INCOME SIDE VARIABLES BY DEFERR
06740     C    ---------------------------------------------------------------
06750              FINT(T)=FINT(T)*DEFERR(T)
06760              FSURP(T)=FSURP(T)*DEFERR(T)
06770              IBT(T)=IBT(T)*DEFERR(T)
06780              PINT(T)=PINT(T)*DEFERR(T)
06790              SSURPE(T)=SSURPE(T)*DEFERR(T)
06800              STPNIA(T)=STPNIA(T)*DEFERR(T)
```

```
06810          CCF(T)=CCF(T)*DEFERR(T)
06820          CHI(T)=CHI(T)*DEFERR(T)
06830          COASDI(T)=COASDI(T)*DEFERR(T)
06840          CSI(T)=CSI(T)*DEFERR(T)
06850          DIV(T)=DIV(T)*DEFERR(T)
06860          DPY(T)=DPY(T)*DEFERR(T)
06870          FCSI(T)=FCSI(T)*DEFERR(T)
06880          FFA(T)=FFA(T)*DEFERR(T)
06890          FIBT(T)=FIBT(T)*DEFERR(T)
06900          FTPNIA(T)=FTPNIA(T)*DEFERR(T)
06910          FTRF(T)=FTRF(T)*DEFERR(T)
06920          INT(T)=INT(T)*DEFERR(T)
06930          NCCCA(T)=NCCCA(T)*DEFERR(T)
06940          PCSI(T)=PCSI(T)*DEFERR(T)
06950          PERSAV(T)=PERSAV(T)*DEFERR(T)
06960          SCSI(T)=SCSI(T)*DEFERR(T)
06970          SIBT(T)=SIBT(T)*DEFERR(T)
06980          SPT(T)=SPT(T)*DEFERR(T)
06990          STRF(T)=STRF(T)*DEFERR(T)
07000          STRFO(T)=STRFO(T)*DEFERR(T)
07010          SUBLS(T)=SUBLS(T)*DEFERR(T)
07020          TPSOI(T)=TPSOI(T)*DEFERR(T)
07030          TRF(T)=TRF(T)*DEFERR(T)
07040          TRF3(T)=TRF3(T)*DEFERR(T)
07050          YPT(T)=YPT(T)*DEFERR(T)
07060    C     -------------------------------------------------------------
07070    C     ******ADJUST PRODUCT SIDE VARIABLES BY DEFERR
07080    C     -------------------------------------------------------------
07090          INVIN(T)=INVIN(T)*DEFERR(T)
07100          RCIN(T)=RCIN(T)*DEFERR(T)
07110          PCEN(T)=PCEN(T)*DEFERR(T)
07120          PSN(T)=PSN(T)*DEFERR(T)
07130          PDEN(T)=PDEN(T)*DEFERR(T)
07140          XPTN(T)=XPTN(T)*DEFERR(T)
07150          MPTN(T)=MPTN(T)*DEFERR(T)
07160          SPRN(T)=SPRN(T)*DEFERR(T)
07170          FPRDFN(T)=FPRDFN(T)*DEFERR(T)
07180          FPRON(T)=FPRON(T)*DEFERR(T)
07190          FPRN(T)=FPRN(T)*DEFERR(T)
07200          NETXMN(T)=NETXMN(T)*DEFERR(T)
07210          BFIN(T)=PSN(T)+PDEN(T)
07220          NPTN(T)=GAPN(T)*C7/C3
07230          NPT(T)=NPTN(T)/(PCED(T)*DEFERR(T))
07240          VATRN(T)=NPTN(T)/PCEN(T)
07250          VATR(T)=VATRN(T)
07260    C     -------------------------------------------------------------
07270    C     ******CALCULATE REMAINNING CORPORATE VARIABLES
07280    C     -------------------------------------------------------------
07290          CCCA(T)=CCF(T)*(CCCAR+DEPA(T))
07300          CIVA(T)=CIVA71*G3**TLAG
07310          CP(T)=CCF(T)-CCCA(T)-CIVA(T)
07320          FCT(T)=TRC(T)*CP(T)-ITC(T)*0.041*PDEN(T)
07330          SCT(T)=4.3*(1.0+1.2*G5)**TLAG
07340    C     -------------------------------------------------------------
07350    C     ******PERSONAL CONSUMPTION STATISTICS
07360    C     -------------------------------------------------------------
07370          PCEG(T)=PCE(T)-GAP(T)
07380          PCEPC(T)=(PCE(T)/POP(T))*1000000.0
07390          PCEPCG(T)=(PCEG(T)/POP(T))*1000000.0
07400          PCER(T)=PCE(T)/GNP(T)
07410          PCERG(T)=PCEG(T)/GNP(T)
```

```
07420          GPCEPC(T)=PCEPC(T)/PCEPC(T-1)
07430          GPCEPG(T)=PCEPCG(T)/PCEPCG(T-1)
07440    C     -------------------------------------------------------------
07450    C     ******WRAPUP CALCULATIONS
07460    C     -------------------------------------------------------------
07470          TOTL3R(T)=FTPNIA(T)+FCSI(T)+FCT(T)+FIBT(T)
07480          TOTL3E(T)=FPRN(T)+TRF3(T)+GRNTS(T)+FSURLS(T)+FINT(T)
07490          FSURP(T)=TOTL3R(T)-TOTL3E(T)
07500          SURP(T)=FSURP(T)+NPTN(T)
07510          NNP(T)=GNPN(T)-NCCCA(T)-CCCA(T)
07520          CPCIVA(T)=CP(T)+CIVA(T)
07530          TPNIA(T)=FTPNIA(T)+STPNIA(T)
07540          TOTL5R(T)=STPNIA(T)+SIBT(T)+SCT(T)+SCSI(T)+GRNTS(T)
07550          TOTL5E(T)=SPRN(T)+STRF(T)+SINT(T)-SSURPE(T)
07560          SSURP(T)=TOTL5R(T)-TOTL5E(T)
07570          UNDCP(T)=CP(T)-DIV(T)-FCT(T)-SCT(T)
07580          TOTL6S(T)=PERSAV(T)+UNDCP(T)+CIVA(T)+CCCA(T)+NCCCA(T)
07590          GSURP(T)=FSURP(T)+SSURP(T)
07600          GI(T)=RCIN(T)+INVIN(T)+BFIN(T)
07610    C     -------------------------------------------------------------
07620    C     ******SETUP OUTPUT ARRAYS
07630    C     -------------------------------------------------------------
07640          OPS(T,1)=GNP(T)
07650          OPS(T,2)=PCE(T)
07660          OPS(T,3)=BFI(T)
07670          OPS(T,4)=INVI(T)
07680          OPS(T,5)=RCI(T)
07690          OPS(T,6)=NETXM(T)
07700          OPS(T,7)=FPR(T)
07710          OPS(T,8)=FPRDF(T)
07720          OPS(T,9)=FPRO(T)
07730          OPS(T,10)=SPR(T)
07740          OPS(T,11)=FD(T)
07750          OPS(T,12)=GAP(T)
07760          OPS(T,13)=NPT(T)
07770          OPS(T,14)=VATR(T)
07780          OPSN(T,1)=GNPN(T)
07790          OPSN(T,2)=PCEN(T)
07800          OPSN(T,3)=BFIN(T)
07810          OPSN(T,4)=INVIN(T)
07820          OPSN(T,5)=RCIN(T)
07830          OPSN(T,6)=NETXMN(T)
07840          OPSN(T,7)=FPRN(T)
07850          OPSN(T,8)=FPRDFN(T)
07860          OPSN(T,9)=FPRON(T)
07870          OPSN(T,10)=SPRN(T)
07880          OPSN(T,11)=FDN(T)
07890          OPSN(T,12)=GAPN(T)
07900          OPSN(T,13)=NPTN(T)
07910          OPSN(T,14)=VATRN(T)
07920          FB(T,1)=FTPNIA(T)
07930          FB(T,2)=FCSI(T)
07940          FB(T,3)=FCT(T)
07950          FB(T,4)=FIBT(T)
07960          FB(T,5)=TOTL3R(T)
07970          FB(T,6)=FPRN(T)
07980          FB(T,7)=FPRDFN(T)
07990          FB(T,8)=FPRON(T)
08000          FB(T,9)=TRF3(T)
08010          FB(T,10)=FTRF(T)
08020          FB(T,11)=FFA(T)
```

```
08030            FB(T,12)=GRNTS(T)
08040            FB(T,13)=FSUBLS(T)
08050            FB(T,14)=FINT(T)
08060            FB(T,15)=TOTL3E(T)
08070            FB(T,16)=FSURP(T)
08080            FB(T,17)=SURP(T)
08090            IS(T,1)=GNPN(T)
08100            IS(T,2)=NCCCA(T)
08110            IS(T,3)=CCCA(T)
08120            IS(T,4)=NNP(T)
08130            IS(T,5)=CSI(T)
08140            IS(T,6)=FCSI(T)
08150            IS(T,7)=SCSI(T)
08160            IS(T,8)=CPCIVA(T)
08170            IS(T,9)=SUBLS(T)
08180            IS(T,10)=IBT(T)
08190            IS(T,11)=FIBT(T)
08200            IS(T,12)=SIBT(T)
08210            IS(T,13)=DIV(T)
08220            IS(T,14)=INT(T)
08230            IS(T,15)=PINT(T)
08240            IS(T,16)=FINT(T)
08250            IS(T,17)=SINT(T)
08260            IS(T,18)=TRF(T)
08270            IS(T,19)=FTRF(T)
08280            IS(T,20)=STRF(T)
08290            IS(T,21)=TPNIA(T)
08300            IS(T,22)=FTPNIA(T)
08310            IS(T,23)=STPNIA(T)
08320            IS(T,24)=OPY(T)
08330            SLB(T,1)=STPNIA(T)
08340            SLB(T,2)=SIBT(T)
08350            SLB(T,3)=SCT(T)
08360            SLB(T,4)=SCSI(T)
08370            SLB(T,5)=GRNTS(T)
08380            SLB(T,6)=TOTL5R(T)
08390            SLB(T,7)=SPRN(T)
08400            SLB(T,8)=STRF(T)
08410            SLB(T,9)=SINT(T)
08420            SLB(T,10)=SSURPE(T)
08430            SLB(T,11)=TOTL5E(T)
08440            SLB(T,12)=SSURP(T)
08450            SIB(T,1)=PERSAV(T)
08460            SIB(T,2)=UNDCP(T)
08470            SIB(T,3)=CIVA(T)
08480            SIB(T,4)=CCCA(T)
08490            SIB(T,5)=NCCCA(T)
08500            SIB(T,6)=TOTL6S(T)
08510            SIB(T,7)=GSURP(T)
08520            SIB(T,8)=GI(T)
08530            PCS(T,1)=PCE(T)
08540            PCS(T,2)=PCEPC(T)
08550            PCS(T,3)=GPCEPC(T)
08560            PCS(T,4)=PCER(T)
08570            PCS(T,5)=PCEG(T)
08580            PCS(T,6)=PCEPCG(T)
08590            PCS(T,7)=GPCEPG(T)
08600            PCS(T,8)=PCERG(T)
08610        195 CONTINUE
08620      C     ----------------------------------------------------------------
08630      C     ******TABLE 1
```

```
08640  C           ----------------------------------------------------------------
08650      199 PAGE=PAGE+1
08660          WRITE(NP,200) TITLE,DATE,PAGE
08670      200 FORMAT(1X,71(1H-),/1X,12A4,1A8,8X,5HPAGE ,I2,///)
08680          WRITE(NP,201) (TAB1(1,I),I=1,5),(J,J=NYB,NYF)
08690      201 FORMAT(16X,5A8,//25X,5(3X,3H197,I1,1X),3X,3H198,I1,1X,//)
08700          DO 204 I=1,13
08710          WRITE(NP,202) (SUB1(I,J),J=1,3),(OPS(K,I),K=NYB,NYF)
08720      202 FORMAT(1X,3A8,6(2X,F6.1))
08730          IF(I .EQ. 1 .OR. I .EQ. 11 .OR. I .EQ. 12)WRITE(NP,203)
08740      203 FORMAT(1H0)
08750      204 CONTINUE
08760          WRITE(NP,198) (SUB1(14,J),J=1,3),(OPS(K,14),K=NYB,NYF)
08770      198 FORMAT(1X,3A8,6(2X,F6.4))
08780          WRITE(NP,205)
08790      205 FORMAT(1X,7(/))
08800  C           ----------------------------------------------------------------
08810  C           ******TABLE 2
08820  C           ----------------------------------------------------------------
08830          WRITE(NP,201) (TAB1(2,I),I=1,5),(J,J=NYB,NYF)
08840          DO 206 I=1,13
08850          WRITE(NP,202) (SUB1(I,J),J=1,3),(OPSN(K,I),K=NYB,NYF)
08860          IF(I .EQ. 1 .OR. I .EQ. 11 .OR. I .EQ. 12)WRITE(NP,203)
08870      206 CONTINUE
08880          WRITE(NP,198) (SUB1(14,J),J=1,3),(OPSN(K,14),K=NYB,NYF)
08890          WRITE(NP,207)
08900      207 FORMAT(1X,3(/))
08910  C           ----------------------------------------------------------------
08920  C           ******TABLE 3
08930  C           ----------------------------------------------------------------
08940          PAGE=PAGE+1
08950          WRITE(NP,200) TITLE,DATE,PAGE
08960          WRITE(NP,201) (TAB1(3,I),I=1,5),(J,J=NYB,NYF)
08970          DO 210 I=1,17
08980          IF(I .EQ. 1)WRITE(NP,208)
08990          IF(I .EQ. 6)WRITE(NP,209)
09000      208 FORMAT(1H0,9HRECIEPTS )
09010      209 FORMAT(1H0,13HEXPENDITURES )
09020          WRITE(NP,202) (SUB2(I,J),J=1,3),(FB(K,I),K=NYB,NYF)
09030          IF(I .EQ.15)WRITE(NP,203)
09040      210 CONTINUE
09050          WRITE(NP,211)
09060      211 FORMAT(1X,33(/))
09070  C           ----------------------------------------------------------------
09080  C           ******TABLE 4
09090  C           ----------------------------------------------------------------
09100          PAGE=PAGE+1
09110          WRITE(NP,200) TITLE,DATE,PAGE
09120          WRITE(NP,201) (TAB1(4,I),I=1,5),(J,J=NYB,NYF)
09130          DO 212 I=1,24
09140          WRITE(NP,202) (SUB3(I,J),J=1,3),(IS(K,I),K=NYB,NYF)
09150          IF(I .EQ. 3 .OR. I .EQ. 4 .OR. I .EQ. 23)WRITE(NP,203)
09160      212 CONTINUE
09170          WRITE(NP,221)
09180      221 FORMAT(1X,26(/))
09190  C           ----------------------------------------------------------------
09200  C           ******TABLE 5
09210  C           ----------------------------------------------------------------
09220          PAGE=PAGE+1
09230          WRITE(NP,200) TITLE,DATE,PAGE
09240          WRITE(NP,201) (TAB1(5,I),I=1,5),(J,J=NYB,NYF)
```

```
09250          DO 213 I=1,12
09260          IF(I ,EQ, 1)WRITE(NP,208)
09270          IF(I ,EQ, 7)WRITE(NP,209)
09280          WRITE(NP,202) (SUB4(I,J),J=1,3),(SLB(K,I),K=NYB,NYF)
09290          IF(I ,EQ, 11)WRITE(NP,203)
09300      213 CONTINUE
09310          WRITE(NP,207)
09320    C     ----------------------------------------------------------------
09330    C     ******TABLE 6
09340    C     ----------------------------------------------------------------
09350          WRITE(NP,201) (TAB1(6,I),I=1,5),(J,J=NYB,NYF)
09360          DO 215 I=1,8
09370          IF(I ,EQ. 1)WRITE(NP,214)
09380      214 FORMAT(1X,21HGROSS PRIVATE SAVING )
09390          WRITE(NP,202) (SUB5(I,J),J=1,3),(SIB(K,I),K=NYB,NYF)
09400          IF(I ,EQ, 6 ,OR, I ,EQ, 7)WRITE(NP,203)
09410      215 CONTINUE
09420          WRITE(NP,216)
09430      216 FORMAT(1X,15(/))
09440    C     ----------------------------------------------------------------
09450    C     ******TABLE 7
09460    C     ----------------------------------------------------------------
09470          PAGE=PAGE+1
09480          WRITE(NP,200) TITLE,DATE,PAGE
09490          WRITE(NP,201) (TAB1(7,I),I=1,5),(J,J=NYB,NYF)
09500          DO 219 I=1,8
09510          IF(I ,EQ. 1)WRITE(NP,217)
09520          IF(I ,EQ. 5)WRITE(NP,218)
09530      217 FORMAT(19H0WITH GAP UNFILLED )
09540      218 FORMAT(32H0WITH GAP FILLED BY CONSUMPTION )
09550          IF(I ,EQ. 3 ,OR, I ,EQ. 7)GO TO 270
09560          IF(I ,EQ. 4 ,OR, I ,EQ. 8)GO TO 270
09570          WRITE(NP,202) (SUB6(I,J),J=1,3),(PCS(K,I),K=NYB,NYF)
09580          GO TO 219
09590      270 WRITE(NP,198) (SUB6(I,J),J=1,3),(PCS(K,I),K=NYB,NYF)
09600      219 CONTINUE
09610          WRITE(NP,220)
09620      220 FORMAT(1X,45(/),1X,71(1H-))
09630    C     ----------------------------------------------------------------
09640    C     ******TRACE ENDOGENOUS VARIABLES
09650    C     ----------------------------------------------------------------
09660          WRITE(NP,5) (TAB2(12,I),I=1,NF4)
09670          READ(NR,6) REPLY
09680          IF(REPLY ,EQ, NO)GO TO 260
09690          WRITE(NP,5) (TAB2(13,I),I=1,NF4)
09700          READ(NR,224) J1,J2
09710      224 FORMAT(I2,1H ,I2)
09720          J2=J2-J1
09730          J1=J1-71
09740      280 WRITE(NP,5) (TAB2(14,I),I=1,NF3)
09750          WRITE(NP,5) (TAB2(15,I),I=1,4)
09760          PAGE=PAGE+1
09770          WRITE(NP,200) TITLE,DATE,PAGE
09780          LINE=4
09790          SW=0
09800          K=0
09810          I=1
09820      225 WRITE(NP,287)
09830      287 FORMAT(1H0)
09840          READ(NR,230) LABEL
09850      232 FORMAT(1A8)
```

```
09860          LINE=LINE+2
09870          IF(LABEL .EQ. FINISH)GO TO 260
09880          IF(LABEL .NE. ALL)GO TO 235
09890          SW=1
09900          GO TO 250
09910    235 IF(I .LE. 125)GO TO 240
09920          I=1
09930    240 IF(I .NE. K)GO TO 242
09940    238 WRITE(NP,241) LABEL
09950    241 FORMAT(1X,1A8,20HNOT FOUND, TRY AGAIN)
09960          LINE=LINE+1
09970          I=I+1
09980          GO TO 225
09990    242 IF(LABEL .EQ. LAB(I))GO TO 243
10000          I=I+1
10010          IF(I .LE. 125)GO TO 235
10020          I=1
10030          GO TO 238
10040    243 K=I
10050    244 K1=INDEX(I)+J1
10060          K2=K1+J2
10070          IF(I .GE. 107)GO TO 281
10080          IF(I .EQ. 51)GO TO 283
10090          IF(I .EQ. 80 .OR. I .EQ. 81)GO TO 283
10100          IF(I .EQ. 83 .OR. I .EQ. 84)GO TO 283
10110          IF( I .EQ. 54 .OR. I .EQ. 68)GO TO 289
10120          IF(I .EQ. 77 .OR. I .EQ. 87)GO TO 289
10130          WRITE(NP,245) (X(J),J=K1,K2)
10140    245 FORMAT(2H+ ,10(1X,F6.1))
10150          GO TO 285
10160    281 WRITE(NP,282) (X(J),J=K1,K2)
10170    282 FORMAT(2H+ ,10(1X,F6.2))
10180          GO TO 285
10190    283 WRITE(NP,284) (X(J),J=K1,K2)
```

```
10200        284 FORMAT(2H+ ,10(1X,F6.4))
10210            GO TO 285        -
10220        289 WRITE(NP,288) (X(J),J=K1,K2)
10230        288 FORMAT(2H+ ,10(1X,F6.0))
10240        285 I=I+1
10250            LINE=LINE+1
10260            IF(LINE .LT. 66)GO TO 286
10270            PAGE=PAGE+1
10280            WRITE(NP,270) TITLE,DATE,PAGE
10290            LINE=4
10300        286 IF(SW .NE. 0)GO TO 250
10310            GO TO 225
10320        252 IF(I .GT. 125)GO TO 283
10330            WRITE(NP,255) LAB(I)
10340        255 FORMAT(/1X,1A8,/)
10350            LINE=LINE+2
10360            GO TO 244
10370     C      ------------------------------------------------------------------
10380     C      ******LAST RUN?
10390     C      ------------------------------------------------------------------
10400        263 WRITE(NP,5) (TAB2(16,I),I=1,NF1)
10410            WRITE(NP,3)
10420            READ(NR,6) REPLY
10430            IF(REPLY .NE. NO)STOP
10440            RUN=RUN+1
10450            GO TO 1
10460            END
```

110

NOTES

NOTES TO CHAPTER 1

[1] For a more complete introduction to the accounts, see William H. Branson, *Macroeconomic Theory and Policy* (New York: Harper & Row, 1972).

[2] Note that transfer payments "to foreigners" are *not* netted against total receipts since these payments do not directly re-enter the U.S. income flow.

[3] Much of this and the following section is based on an unpublished Council of Economic Adviser's Memorandum, William H. Branson, W. Donald Dresser, David J. Ott, Mary Proctor, "A Model for Resource Allocation and Output Distribution," July 21, 1969.

[4] Arthur M. Okun, "The Gap Between Actual and Potential Output," in *The Battle Against Unemployment,* ed. Arthur Okun (New York: W.W. Norton & Co., Inc., 1965), pp. 13-22.

[5] Productivity growth in the public sector is definitionally zero in the NIA, since public sector product is measured by input.

[6] See, for example, the *Economic Report of the President*, 1970 (Washington, D.C.: U.S. Government Printing Office), and Charles L. Schultze, Edward Fried, Alice Rivlen, Nancy H. Teeters, *Setting National Priorities: The 1973 Budget* (Washington, D.C.: The Brookings Institution, 1972).

[7] For an example of the econometric evidence, see Robert J. Gordon, "Inflation in Recession and Recovery," *Brookings Papers on Economic Activity*, no. 2 (1970).

[8] For a discussion of this model, see Lester C. Thurow, "A Medium-term Fiscal Policy Model," *Survey of Current Business*, June 1969.

[9] A more detailed discussion of the role of monetary policy in the AEI budget model is presented on p. 13 below.

[10] *Survey of Current Business*, July 1972.

[11] U.S. Department of Commerce, Bureau of the Census, *Current Population Reports*, Series P-25, No. 473 (January 1972) and No. 476 (February 1972).

[12] William H. Branson, "The Trade Effects of the 1971 Currency Realignments," *Brookings Papers on Economic Activity*, no. 1 (1972).

[13] The results here are not particularly sensitive to the inflation assumption because when disposable personal income in current dollars is derived, it is re-deflated to obtain real income. Thus a higher inflation assumption would raise the nominal GNP estimate at the top of Table 3, but it would also deflate the nominal DPY estimate at the bottom by the same larger percentage.

[14] David J. Ott et al., *Nixon, McGovern, and the Federal Budget.*

[15] Note that if the gap is negative by, say, $5 billion, then actual *realized* aggregate demand will in fact fall short of potential output by perhaps $10-15 billion because consumer expenditure will fall below the projection since GNP will be less than potential GNP. Thus the gap gives the amount of "exogenous" change in demand needed to hold GNP equal to potential GNP.

[16] This is the well-known balanced budget multiplier at work. See William H. Branson, *Macroeconomic Theory and Policy.*

[17] See ibid., Chapters 18 and 22, for discussion of these values.

NOTES TO CHAPTER 2

[18] See Chapter 3 for the projected values of all parameters that were used in the model. The sources of the labor force projections are based on Census Series E projections for 1975 and 1980; the intermediate years were interpolated from a trend line consistent with these benchmarks.

In the AEI model, the 3 percent drop in real GNP for each one percentage point excess of the unemployment rate (UR) over 4 percent involves setting $TLF = TLF [1+2(UR-.04)]$. Using a multiplicative factor of 3 produces a drop in GNP of about 5 percent when the unemployment rate is 5 percent, since all of the reduction in employment comes out of the private sector, where GNP per worker is highest. It should also be noted that the model does not "work" for years where actual data are known since the actual labor force will be arbitrarily reduced by the "Okun's Law" assumption. However, it does work properly for a 4 percent unemployment rate year where no adjustment to TLF is made.

[19] The rate of growth of productivity was set at the standard 3 percent, which was also the rate used in the Brookings study by Charles Schultze et al., *Setting National Priorities.* The unemployment rate and the inflation rate were chosen to be consistent with the current objectives of the administration (whether or not they are an economically feasible combination).

[20] 4,142 thousand for elementary and secondary education, 1,339 thousand for higher education and 4,461 thousand for other general government. From Bureau of the Census, *Public Employment in 1971*, GE 71, No. 1 (April 1972).

[21] 1958 dollars are used because the NIA statistics for output per worker in the private sector are given in 1958 dollars.

[22] Unpublished data, Bureau of Economic Activity, Department of Commerce.

[23] This is consistent with recent data. See Table 3.11, any July issue of the *Survey of Current Business.*

[24] A state and local purchases deflator which is calculated from a regression equation is used to inflate purchases for the purpose of deriving state and local CSI. This expedient is necessitated by the fact that information needed for the equation above has not yet been computed at that stage.

[25] For example, consider a case with a Cobb-Douglas production function $Q=K^{\alpha}L^{1-\alpha}$, where Q is real output and K and L are capital and labor inputs, respectively. The marginal product of capital is given by

$$\frac{\delta Q}{\delta K} = \alpha \frac{Q}{K},$$

which is equal to the real "user cost" of capital c/p, where c is the implicit rental value of capital goods per unit of time. In equilibrium, then,

$$\frac{c}{p} = \alpha \frac{Q}{K}, \quad V = \frac{K}{Q} = \alpha \frac{p}{c},$$

where V is the capital/output ratio. As long as the relative price ration pK is constant, so is V.

[26] Lester C. Thurow, "A Medium-term Fiscal Policy Model," *Survey of Current Business,* June 1969.

[27] The procedures used in converting from the unified budget to the NIA budget are explained in "Options Volume."

[28] U.S. Department of Commerce, Bureau of the Census, *Current Population Reports,* Series P-25, No. 476 (February 1972).

[29] U.S. Department of Commerce, Bureau of the Census, *Current Population Reports,* Series P-25, No. 473 (January 1972).

[30] Note that this procedure permits state and local employment to be projected under any consistent set of exogenous population and school enrollment projections.

[31] This procedure, in which state and local purchases (or expenditures) are projected as a function of changes in workload and changes in the quality of the services provided, has been widely used. See, for example, W. H. Robinson, "Financing State and Local Governments: The Outlook for 1975," presented at the New York Chapter of the American Statistical Association, April 24, 1969. Robinson (and others using this technique) also have an index of price change, which is multiplied times the other indexes used in the AEI model. Since the concern here is with state and local government purchases in constant dollars, however, no price term is needed. The values used in the AEI model for average annual increases in scope and quality were 2.4 percent for elementary and secondary education, 0.9 percent for college education, and 3.5 percent for noneducational functions of state and local governments. These figures were derived from 1954-71 NIA data by Thomas Vasquez of the AEI LRBP staff.

[32] See footnote 20.

[33] William H. Branson, "The Trade Effect of the 1971 Currency Realignments," *Brookings Papers on Economic Activity,* no. 1 (1972).

[34] *Annual Report of the Council of Economic Advisers,* 1971 (Washington, D.C.: U.S. Government Printing Office).

[35] See "Options Volume."

[36] Ibid.

[37] In the modern general equilibrium theory of tax incidence, CCF *after taxes* should be a constant fraction of GNP. However, technical difficulties prevented the specification of the equation in that form. If corporate tax rates were changed greatly, this might make some difference in the results. Changes in depreciation laws would make little difference, however, as both corporate and noncorporate depreciation would be affected by such changes.

[38] See Robinson, "Financing State and Local Governments." See also L.R. Kegan and G.P. Roniger, "The Outlook for State and Local Finance," CED supplementary paper no. 23, *Fiscal Issues in the Future of Federalism* (New York, 1968), pp. 281-83. For a summary of work in this field, the findings of which are generally consistent with the above, see Advisory Commission on Intergovernmental Relations, *State and Local Finances: Significant Features and Suggested Legislation* (Washington, D.C.: U.S. Government Printing Office, 1972), p. 301.

[39] For a detailed discussion of the estimating equations for the personal tax and nontax receipts and the relation between tax liability and receipts, see Appendix A.

[40] The tax file is a stratified sample of approximately 80 thousand returns of individuals filing an income tax return in 1966.

[41] *Survey of Current Business,* July 1972, Tables 3.2 and 3.3.

[42] In running the model under a variety of assumptions, dozens of times, the iterative procedure discussed here always converged within four iterations.

[43] See the discussion in Chapter 3, p. 77, for a detailed explanation of how to interpret the printed GAP. These pages also provide a procedure which enables the user to revise the GAP calculation to account for the user's own assumptions about the disposition of the state and local surplus.

[44] The values for DEFERR, obtained in running the model, ranged, for different years, from 1.0033 to 1.0037. Thus, they were in all cases well below one half of one percent of GNP. This, it would seem, provides some justification for the rather ad hoc procedure used in projecting the deflators for the individual components of GNP.

[45] The Treasury estimates are unpublished. The Commerce estimates are in *Survey of Current Business,* August 1971.

NOTES TO CHAPTER 3

[46] Steps 1 through 4 represent the procedure necessary to initiate a logical connection of a portable terminal with the computer system. These steps will be slightly different for a hardwired terminal or a teletype using a data set.

[47] Valid responses to the messages produced by the AEI model are enclosed in parentheses on the same line as the message except for situations in which the required response is descriptive. For example, see step 2.

[48] When a NO or OK response is required, the program checks to determine if the user entered a response of NO. Therefore the user does not actually have to enter the letters OK for a response of OK but can merely depress the carriage return key [CR] instead.

[49] This, of course, assumes that the functional form of the equation remains unchanged.

[50] Data entry in the manner just described is accomplished by using a NAMELIST read statement within the program. If the user adheres to the documentation just presented, he should not encounter any problems. However, if problems do arise, the user should consult a FORTRAN manual for the proper form required in entering the data.

[51] Some of these appear in the previously presented parameter list and some in the exogenous list. This classification is entirely circumstantial and no real distinction should be read into the fact that the variables are classified in this way.

NOTES TO APPENDIX A

[52] The analysis presented here is developed along the line presented in an article by J. Bennett and B. Riggs, "Forecasting Receipts from the Federal Individual Income Tax," *National Tax Journal,* December 1968, pp. 425-36, and is based on an unpublished paper by J. Scott Turner, Attiat F. Ott, and David J. Ott.

[53] The ratio of $\frac{TPSOI}{AGI}$ has always been less than .193 which makes the right-hand side of the above inequality positive. The calculated value of α_0 is negative which implies equation (A.7) is consistent with a progressive rate structure.

[54] The value of $S(t)$ depends on the changes in the tax code. For example, the 10 percent surtax legislated in 1969 can be easily incorporated by setting $S(69)=.10$. However, nonproportional changes in marginal tax rates or changes in the definition of taxable income require outside calculations of $S(t)$ (by using a sample of individual income tax returns). In the AEI model $[1+S(t)]$ was replaced by the term TS.

[55] A procedure for adjusting the TP(SOI) series to be consistent with 1966 rate structure is given in Bennett and Riggs, "Forecasting Receipts," p. 430.

LIBRARY OF DAVIDSON COLLEGE

Books on regular loan may be checked out for **two weeks.** Books must be presented at the Circulation Desk in order to be renewed.

A fine is charged after date due.

Special books are subject to special regulations at the discretion of library staff.